INVENTING ACADEMIC FREEDOM

THE 1968 STRAX AFFAIR AT THE
UNIVERSITY OF NEW BRUNSWICK

PETER C. KENT

Formac Publishing Company Limited
Halifax

Formac Publishing Company Limited recognizes the support of the Province of Nova Scotia through the Department of Communities, Culture and Heritage. We are pleased to work in partnership with the Culture Division to develop and promote our culture resources for all Nova Scotians. We acknowledge the support of the Canada Council for the Arts which last year invested $24.3 million in writing and publishing throughout Canada. We acknowledge the financial support of the Government of Canada through the Canada Book Fund for our publishing activities.

Cover design: Tyler Cleroux

Library and Archives Canada Cataloguing in Publication

Kent, Peter C., 1938-
  Inventing academic freedom : the 1968 Strax affair at the University of New Brunswick / Peter C. Kent.

Includes bibliographical references and index.
Issued also in electronic formats.
ISBN 978-1-4595-0148-5

1.Strax, Norman. 2.Academic freedom--New Brunswick--History--20th century. 3.University of New Brunswick--Faculty--History--20th century. 4.College teachers--Political activity--New Brunswick--History--20th century. 5.New Brunswick--Politics and government--1952-1970. I.Title.

LC72.5.N49K45 2012 378.1'213097151 C2012-903527-0

Formac Publishing Company Limited
5502 Atlantic Street
Halifax, NS, Canada
B3H 1G4
www.formac.ca

Printed and bound in Canada.

INVENTING ACADEMIC FREEDOM

To Aline and Bill
with all good wishes
for Christmas 2012

Wendy and Peter

Dec 9, 2012

CONTENTS

PREFACE

I was at the centre of the Strax Affair at the University of New Brunswick. In 1968–69, I was a junior member of the history department and worked as executive assistant to President Colin B. Mackay, in whose office I was privy to many of the discussions of strategy and tactics in dealing with the events of the year. At the same time, I was also the don of the MacKenzie House residence, which housed some of the leading student activists and politicians. The story of the Strax Affair has remained with me for the past forty years as a living series of events that had a profound influence both on my own outlook and on the development of one of the larger universities of Atlantic Canada. It is a part of the history of UNB that has never really been examined, just as it is part of the story of Canadian universities in the heady days of the radical sixties. It is a story that deserves to be told.

I write about the Strax Affair as a participant historian. I observed many of the events in that year and was well acquainted with most of the players. I tried to balance my friendships with the students and my loyalty to the president and to remain open to both camps. I thought it worked at the time, and like to think I retain an ability to see the conflict from many perspectives. Within ten years of the events of 1968–69, while they were still fresh in my memory, I recorded my memoirs, which have been incorporated into this narrative. Since then, I have reviewed the university archives and interviewed many of the players, so hopefully, my memory has been corrected by the archival sources and by the recollections of others. What I hope my experience will bring to this narrative is the colouring of my own impressions and feelings about the individuals and the situations involved.

University of New Brunswick

My thanks are due to President Elizabeth Parr-Johnston, who authorized my access to the presidential papers in the UNB Archives and to the archivists Linda Baier, Mary Flagg and Patti Johnson for their assistance. The book would not have been possible without the willingness of the following individuals to be interviewed and to dredge up their sometimes vivid recollections of that period: Alwyn Berland, Alan Borovoy, Ann Cameron, David Cox, Kenneth Cox, John Earl, Gertrude Gunn, Lawson Hunter, David Jonah, Lynn McDonald, Tom Murphy, John Oliver, Stephen Patterson, Marion Rogers, Harold Sharp, Michael Start, Dan Weston and Murray Young. The late Gordon Fairweather and the late Leslie Shemilt provided me with particularly insightful interviews, and I only regret that they did not live to see the finished book.

My thanks must also go to Franz Martin, a teacher in California, who attended UNB on exchange in 1968–69, participated in the demonstrations of that year and kept a daily journal of his impression of events. When Franz learned that I was working on a book about the Strax Affair, he sent me his journal and invited me to make use of it.

Thanks to Bill Seabrook, Ted Colson, Doug Brewer and Joy Cummings for providing me with photographs to use in the book.

In preparing the final version of the manuscript, I have had assistance and advice from friends and colleagues David Bell, Tom Condon, Margaret Conrad, Linda and Greg Kealey, Sean Kennedy, Susan Montague, David Adams Richards and Steve Turner.

My particular thanks go to my wife Wendy, who has lived with this book throughout the forty-plus years of our marriage. Wendy has read every word and has been one of my harshest critics in identifying infelicities and repetitions. Her support and encouragement have helped me to eventually bring this book to a conclusion.

CAST OF CHARACTERS

THE UNIVERSITY OF NEW BRUNSWICK IN 1968–69

Some Members of the Board of Governors

Sir Max Aitken — Chancellor

Colin B. Mackay — President and Vice-Chancellor, Chair of the Board of Governors

K.C. Irving — Industrialist and government representative from Saint John

Dr. B.L. Jewett — Physician and government representative from Fredericton

Mary Louise Lynch — Lawyer and government representative from Ottawa

Mrs. Howard Rogers — Alumnae representative from East Riverside

Eric Garland — Associate Professor of Civil Engineering

George McAllister — Professor of Law

Leslie W. Shemilt — Professor of Chemical Engineering

D. Murray Young — Professor of History

The Administration

Colin B. Mackay — President and Vice-Chancellor

Alfred G. Bailey — Vice-President (Academic) and Head of the History Department

Beverley Macaulay — Vice-President (Administration)

W.C. Desmond Pacey — Dean of Graduate Studies and Head of the English Department

W. Stewart MacNutt — Dean of Arts

C. William Argue — Dean of Science and Head of the Biology Department

James O. Dineen — Dean of Engineering and Head of the Department of Electrical Engineering
William F. Ryan — Dean of Law
Gertrude Gunn — University Librarian
Chester Mahan — University Comptroller
Brigadier A.F.B. Knight — Director of Personnel
Charles Barnett — Chief of Security
Alan Pacey — Director of Information
Roberta Weiner — Head of the Circulation Department in the Library
Isabel "Byng" McKay — Secretary to the President
Peter C. Kent — Assistant to the President

Members of Faculty

Dugald Blue — Associate Professor of Education, Registrar and Dean of Student Services
Allen Boone — Professor of Physics and Head of the Department
Doug Brewer — Associate Professor of Chemistry
Phil Buckner — Lecturer in History and Don of Neville House
Ann Cameron — Lecturer in Psychology
Don Cameron — Lecturer in English
Jim Chapman — Professor of History
John Earl — Associate Professor of Economics
Eric Garland — Associate Professor of Civil Engineering and member of the Board of Governors
Peter C. Kent — Lecturer in History, Assistant to the President and Don of MacKenzie House
Gottfried Konecny — Professor of Surveying Engineering and Head of the Department of Surveying Engineering
Peter MacRae — Lecturer in Sociology and Don of Aitken House
Ed Maher — Professor of Business Administration and Head of the Department
George McAllister — Professor of Law and member of the Board of Governors

Brent McKeown — Lecturer in Sociology and Acting Dean of Men's Residences

George Mossman — General Secretary of the Student Christian Movement

Gordon Myers — Director of Student Aid and Don of Bridges House

Gerald Pacholke — Lecturer in Mathematics

Stephen Patterson — Assistant Professor of History

Doug Pullman — Professor of Sociology and Head of the Department of Sociology and Anthropology

Perry Robinson — Professor of Philosophy and Head of the Department

Doug Ruthven — Assistant Professor of Chemical Engineering and Don of Jones House

Harold Sharp — Associate Professor of Business Administration

Leslie W. Shemilt — Professor of Chemical Engineering, Head of the Department and member of the Board of Governors

Norman Strax — Assistant Professor of Physics

Kent Thompson — Assistant Professor of English

Israel Unger — Assistant Professor of Chemistry

Theo Weiner — Associate Professor of Physics

Richard Wilbur — Associate Professor of History

D. Murray Young — Professor of History and member of the Board of Governors

Students

Nelson Adams — Fredericton, graduate student in Classics

Richard Archer — Fredericton, student at Teachers' College

Wayne Beach — Toronto, Student's Representative Council President 1967–68

Clayton Burns — Fredericton, English student

David Cox — Saint John, Electrical Engineering student and Student's Representative Council President 1968

Frank Goldspink — News Editor at the *Brunswickan*

Geoffrey Green — Student's Representative Council President 1968, Psychology student

David Hallam — Montreal, Philosophy student

Lawson Hunter — Florenceville, NB, Student's Representative Council President 1966–67, Law student and Proctor in MacKenzie House

Dave Jonah — Moncton, Arts student

Dan Lingemann — History student

Franz Martin — Exchange Student (of History) from the University of Maine (Orono)

Bronwyn McIntyre — Saint John, History student

Tom Murphy — Fredericton, Sociology student

Tom Murray — Fredericton, Engineering student

Hart North — Toronto, Arts student and chair of the 1968 Orientation Committee

John Oliver — Marysville, NB, Economics student, Editor of the *Brunswickan*, 1968–69

Alastair Robertson — Scotland, graduate student in English, Acting Student's Representative Council President 1968–69

Michael Start — Fredericton, Arts student, Student's Representative Council President 1969–70

Dan Weston — Oromocto, Arts student

Faculty and Administrators of the Past and Future

Lord Beaverbrook — Honorary Chancellor 1953–64

Norman Mackenzie — President and Vice-Chancellor, 1940–44, subsequently President of the University of British Columbia

Albert Truman — President and Vice-Chancellor 1948–53

Francis J. Toole — Professor of Chemistry, Dean of Graduate Studies, Vice-President (Academic); retired in 1967

Reuben Rosenberg — Professor of Mathematics and Head of the Department; left UNB in 1967

James O. Dineen — President and Vice-Chancellor 1969–72

W.C. Desmond Pacey — Acting President 1972

John Anderson — President and Vice-Chancellor 1973–79

Thomas J. Condon — Acting President 1979–80

James Downey — President and Vice-Chancellor 1980–90, subsequently President of the University of Waterloo

NEW BRUNSWICK AND CANADA

Howard Adelman — Initiator of Rochdale College, Toronto

Willard Allen — President of the Canadian Association of University Teachers 1969–70

S.C. Atkinson — Governor of the University of Saskatchewan

Justice J. Paul Barry — Saint John, Queen's Bench Division of the Supreme Court of New Brunswick

Alwyn Berland — Executive Secretary of the Canadian Association of University Teachers from 1969

Alan Borovoy — General Counsel, Canadian Civil Liberties Association, Toronto

Chief Justice G.F.G. Bridges — New Brunswick Court of Queen's Bench

J. Edward Byrne — Bathurst lawyer, chair of the New Brunswick Royal Commission on Municipal Finance and Taxation

Ken Cox — President of NBTel

John J. Deutsch — Vice-Principal (Administration) of Queen's University, Chair of the Royal Commissions on Higher Education in New Brunswick

Gordon Fairweather — Member of Parliament for Fundy-Royal, 1962–77

Hugh John Flemming — Premier of New Brunswick, 1952–60

Don Gilliss — Lawyer, Saint John

Duff Harper — Lawyer, Fredericton

Richard Hatfield — Premier of New Brunswick, 1970–87

William Hoyt — Lawyer, Fredericton

Vincent Kelly — Lawyer, Toronto

Justice R.V. Limerick — New Brunswick Court of Queen's Bench

Colin and Jeanette Mackay — Saint John, parents of Colin B. Mackay

Hugh Mackay — Saint John, uncle of Colin B. Mackay

Wallace and Harrison McCain — Florenceville industrialists

Lynn McDonald — Assistant Professor of Sociology, University of Western Ontario

C. Brough Macpherson — University of Toronto, President of the Canadian Association of University Teachers, 1968–69

Professor Arthur Meagher — Faculty of Law, Dalhousie University

J.B. Milner — Chair, Academic Freedom and Tenure Committee, Canadian Association of University Teachers

David C. Nicholson — Lawyer, Fredericton

James F. O'Sullivan — Secretary to the Byrne Commission and the two Deutsch Commissions; subsequently Chair, New Brunswick Higher Education Commission

Professor Earl Palmer — Faculty of Law, University of Western Ontario

Justice Lou McC. Ritchie — New Brunswick Court of Queen's Bench

Louis J. Robichaud — Premier of New Brunswick, 1960–70

Hugh Saunderson — President of the University of Manitoba

Murray Sargeant — Fredericton Superintendent of Schools

Lord Hartley Shawcross — Prosecutor at the Nuremberg Trials

Percy Smith — Executive Secretary of the Canadian Association of University Teachers until 1968

J.F.H. Teed — Lawyer, Saint John

John Turner — Federal Minister of Justice

Michael Wardell — Publisher of the Fredericton *Daily Gleaner*

ABBREVIATIONS USED IN THE TEXT

AAUP — American Association of University Professors
AUCC — Association of Universities and Colleges of Canada
AUNBT — Association of University of New Brunswick Teachers
CAUT — Canadian Association of University Teachers
CCLA — Canadian Civil Liberties Association
CUCND — Combined Universities Campaign for Nuclear Disarmament
CUP — Canadian University Press
CUS — Canadian Union of Students
FAPO — Fredericton Anti-Poverty Organization
SCM — Student Christian Movement
SDS — Students for a Democratic Society
SDU — Students for a Democratic University (at McGill and Simon Fraser)
SRC — Student's Representative Council
SUPA — Student Union for Peace Action
UBC — University of British Columbia
UGEQ — Union générale des étudiants de Québec
UNB — University of New Brunswick

Chapter 1

"LET'S PLAY BOOKIE-BOOK"

"FUCK THE ID CARDS" screamed the mimeographed broadsheet that I pulled from my car window on the morning of Friday, September 20, 1968. The fall term of 1968–69 at the University of New Brunswick had just started, and I was beginning my fourth year as a lecturer in history and don of the MacKenzie House men's residence. I was also entering my second year as executive assistant to President Colin B. Mackay.

The broadsheet told us that "the cats that control this place — K.C. Irving, Colin B. Mackay, etc. — have a new gimmick this year: ID CARDS! The security will be tight just like at an H-bomb factory." It then went on to explain why photo-ID cards were being introduced:

> *(1) The cards will help Colin B. suppress student-faculty insurrections, and thus help him to stop us from building a democratic university.*

> *(2) The cards will help the rent-a-cops kick out our non-student brothers from the stud and the campus.*

Colin wants to keep UNB people isolated from the community at large, and thus help to keep both the students and the community powerless to change the present businessman-dominated university administration.

(3) ID cards help to make people feel and act like powerless sheep.

We were invited to fight the ID cards by refusing to have our photos taken, by burning the cards and by refusing to show them to any Campus Security personnel who asked for them. "If Colin and Irving don't chuck the whole police state ID card bit, we'll be forced to take direct militant action. We'll do whatever's necessary to fuck up the card system and the police shit."[1]

This was not the normal style of discourse at UNB in the 1960s, particularly in its administrative offices. Later that day, I went to the president's office, where his secretary asked me to take a copy of the broadsheet to Gertude Gunn, the chief librarian, who hadn't yet seen it. I put it inside a blank file folder, as if taking her a dirty book in a plain brown envelope.

Before the day was out, the "direct militant action" had been launched at the Harriet Irving Library. The library had been opened in the spring of 1968 and had been named after the wife of New Brunswick industrialist K.C. Irving, who had chaired the fundraising campaign. The demonstration began at 6:00 pm, when Norman Strax, an assistant professor of physics, along with David Hallam, a philosophy student from Montreal, and Clayton Burns, an English student from Fredericton, arrived at the circulation desk of the library with "armloads of books from the stacks." When asked to show their ID cards, they refused, and the staff, in turn, refused to let the students take out the books. The books were left on the circulation desk and the protestors returned to the stacks for more. In recognition of the fact that Strax was a faculty member, he was allowed to sign out five books without his ID card, but, "it being abundantly evident that his lack of a card was not an oversight but a provocation," all further loans to him were also denied. The demonstration continued for two hours, during which time 250 volumes were left on the circulation desk. The dean of science came out and "reasoned and remonstrated" with Strax, but to no avail. The librarian eventually closed the library at 8:00 pm.

The proposal for having a general university photo-ID card had first been considered in the fall of 1967, when the engineering faculty had arranged a demonstration of the Polaroid Land camera system, and following this demonstration, the administrative vice-president had convened a meeting of faculty, student and administration representatives, along with representatives from St. Thomas University and the New Brunswick Teachers' College, which both shared the UNB campus. At the meeting, the students showed the greatest interest in having photo-ID cards. The librarian did not feel these cards to be essential, but agreed to adapt the library operation if other sections of the university felt such a system would be a good thing. St. Thomas University and the teachers' college also agreed to go along with the program if UNB decided to proceed.

There had been a residence issue in 1967 over "open rooms," whether men should be allowed to entertain women in their rooms at a limited number of house socials a year. David Cox was a student in electrical engineering who lived in the Neill House men's residence, and in his third year served as president of his house. He was a strong student and an effective house president and had been selected as one of three students on a committee with Mackay to sort out the issue. Cox got along well with Mackay, who really wasn't very interested in the issue but was under pressure to make some kind of a change. As a result of these deliberations, a new "open rooms" policy was introduced in 1967, with some arcane rules about what was and was not permitted when women were visiting the men.

This new policy represented a victory for reformist students who felt they had secured more rights and privileges from the university administration, and Cox acquired a lot of credit for his work on "open rooms." As a result, he was encouraged to run for the presidency of the Student's Representative Council (SRC) in the spring of 1968 by his friends in the engineering faculty, some of whom felt that an engineer as student president would put a brake on some of the radical representatives. He anticipated providing responsible leadership on student issues from a different perspective, believing that "you could build it right of centre as opposed to left of centre and this could be a helpful thing." To his own surprise he won the election, presumably with the support of his own faculty and the residence. As assistant to President Mackay, I made it my job to get to know the campus student leaders and to offer my services as a channel for them to the president. As SRC president, Cox developed an effective relationship with Mackay and with other university administrators. He had a respect for them and yet was also prepared to challenge their views with sound arguments of his own. His relations with his student peers, on the other hand, were less comfortable and I judged that he had little sense of student politics in 1968. I occasionally discussed issues with him during that summer and fall and was repeatedly asking him whether he knew what kind of student support existed for various schemes that he was proposing. He never seemed to know who was with him and who wasn't.

Cox and the SRC executive were interested in photo-ID cards for all the students, which could be useful as passes to dances and athletic events and could secure student discounts where they were available in the city. To help defray the costs, Cox convinced Mackay that the university could also make use of these cards to identify students in residence, the library and at other university functions. It was agreed to split the costs between the SRC and the university,[3] and on August 9 the faculty were informed by the vice-president (academic) that the cards had been "adopted as a convenience by a number of universities" and that from now on all borrowing from the library would require the presentation of the ID card.[4]

In preparation for the use of the ID cards in the library, Roberta Weiner, the head of circulation, had drawn up detailed instructions for the staff of the circulation and reserve desks on how to cope with the new cards. The cards were to be used for the first time on the first day of term, at which time, all faculty and student borrowers were to be asked if they had their ID cards. If they did not have one, they were to be told how and where to get one but were still to be allowed to borrow books without a card. After one week, students without cards could still borrow books, but would have to wait while the librarian checked the library registration cards to make sure they were bona fide students. Even in the case of "well-known eccentric students," who "may be unwilling or unable to present their ID cards properly," librarians were instructed to be generous: "Treating all students alike, you MUST ask for his ID card. But avoid arguments. Do not waste your energies fighting it out. Stamp his registration card each time you lend him books without seeing his ID card."

The only situation in which the staff were not to allow books to be borrowed without a card was in the case of "emphatic protest for the sake of protest," when a "student may say he objects on principle." In such a case: "Avoid argument. Avoid the big fuss that he likely wants to arouse. Keep cool. Just say that, in such a case, your instructions are to refuse to stamp out his books. Tell him he will have to use them within the building...If necessary walk off into the workroom if you have had to refuse to stamp out his books." The names of these students were to be reported to the head of circulation. No provision was made for the case of a protesting faculty member.[5]

*　*　*

The summer of 1968 had been an uneasy one. Riots destroyed the core of many American cities as a result of the Memphis murder of Martin Luther King Jr. in April. At the same time, Columbia University in New York was brought to a halt by massive student demonstrations. Bobby Kennedy, who had been the guest speaker at UNB's fall convocation in October 1967, was assassinated in Los Angeles in June. In Mexico City, the police and army shot rioting students as a prelude to the opening of the summer Olympics. And August saw the Democratic Convention in Chicago and the televised bludgeoning of swarms of demonstrators by Mayor Daley's police.

In Canada, there had been restlessness in a number of universities where students were demanding representation on governing bodies. Radical students at Simon Fraser University had been protesting and demonstrating over local issues since 1966, and in June 1968, after the university had been censured by the Canadian Association of University Teachers (CAUT), students had staged a campus sit-in in protest. At McGill in the winter of 1967–68, Principal H. Rocke Robertson had challenged the editor of the *McGill Daily* over a vulgar article that the students had defended in the interests of press freedom. And in the spring of 1968, a number of black students at Montreal's Sir George Williams University, many from the West Indies, had initiated a series of complaints about the racism of a member of the biology department.

I had anticipated problems at UNB when the fall term opened, and I put my thoughts in a memo to the president during the summer. I had noticed how some of the students, especially those

The author's photo-ID card from 1968.

associated with the on-campus Mobilization Against the War in Vietnam, were taking local issues much more seriously than before and were obviously looking for issues about which to protest. Since the protests and the violence taking place in the rest of the world were in the news and on television daily, it was natural that some attempts would be made to emulate other campuses and other protests. I proposed that some initiative should be taken to resolve obvious problems before they touched off confrontations between students and the administration.

The area that I judged most likely to produce strong reaction and protest from the students was the behaviour of the university's Security Police. The security staff was made up of members of the Canadian Corps of Commissionaires and other individuals hired directly by the university. While some members of the security staff worked in the residences and the library, knew and understood the students and got along well with them, others were assigned to general patrol duty around the campus. While their main assignment was to protect campus property, they frequently interpreted this as giving them authority to order students around, ask them for identification and generally harass them. The tone was set for them by the chief of security, Charles Barnett, the former chief of the Marysville police. Barnett, who was frequently seen on campus wearing an elaborate uniform trimmed with gold braid, demonstrated little understanding of university students and had become a prime target for student ridicule. His negative attitude toward students was, unfortunately, reflected by many members of his staff. In my memo to the president that summer, I stressed the importance of imposing some controls on the behaviour of the Security Police. Mackay never answered my memo or discussed it with me. I believe he was not very happy with Chief Barnett's performance but shied at that time from the difficulties involved in any attempt to control or get rid of him.

The Security Police were not, however, destined to become the central issue. Perhaps they were too obvious a target. The introduction of photo-ID cards passed by unnoticed during the summer and was never, in fact, a contentious issue with the university community until the demonstrators defined it as one in September.

My apprehensions in the summer were shared by a number of other faculty members who sensed the increased seriousness of students about campus issues and also the seeming reluctance of Mackay and the administration to deal with them. We felt there was a need for more discussion among students, faculty and administration lest the university become increasingly polarized, and we set about in the first two weeks of term to do something about it. Brent McKeown, a sociologist, was the acting dean of men's residence and Gordon Myers, the university awards officer, was don of Bridges House. The three of us were good friends and had worked closely with the student Orientation Committee over the previous couple of years in an attempt to replace the hazing of new students with a more realistic introduction to what a university was supposed to be about. This plan included faculty-student discussion groups during orientation week in September. We had hoped to use our influence with the Orientation Committee to stress the idea of the university as an intellectual community in the fall of 1968.

The most visible faculty member at the beginning of September 1968, however, was Kent Thompson of the English department. Thompson believed there was a need to defuse the atmosphere somewhat and planned to organize a general faculty-student-administration meeting where issues could be raised and discussed openly and remedial action could be suggested. Above all, he suggested, we must not take ourselves too seriously. "Everyone needs to laugh a lot more."

A well-attended meeting was held in the theatre of Memorial Hall in early September. Faculty and students raised and discussed issues in a relatively open atmosphere. When it came time to vacate the hall, we adjourned to the front steps, where it was decided to elect a committee to act on the recommendations of the meeting. It was at that meeting that I got a real sense of the seriousness and determination of some of the student leaders and realized that greater polarization existed on campus than I had thought. In choosing a spokesman for the meeting, Thompson called for nominations. Entering into the spirit of the meeting, I nominated Hart North, who had been chairman of the Orientation Committee and was known to me as a sensible and responsible student leader who had also been involved in organizing the Memorial Hall meeting. My nomination was probably the kiss of death for North, who got only one vote — mine — and lost out to Lawson Hunter.

In 1968, Lawson Hunter was the elder statesman of the UNB student body. He had served as SRC president in 1966–67, and since that time had been working to develop co-operative housing at UNB. In both of these projects, he had worked closely and well with Colin Mackay. After he completed his degree in science in 1967, he went on to law school, and in 1968 he became one of the two student proctors in MacKenzie House. Through his work with co-operative housing and with the Canadian Union of Students, Hunter was fully aware of the radicalism that was developing across the country and was sympathetic to it. As radicalism came to UNB, he was in touch with its currents on campus.[5] He was an effective and articulate spokesman for the students, was highly respected and was obviously jockeying for position in that volatile September. Hunter had not been involved in organizing the Memorial Hall meeting, and in fact had not been very evident at the meeting. Yet when the election was being held, he suddenly appeared in the middle of the group on the front steps, was nominated and duly elected.

The "Front Step Committee," as it came to be called, did not achieve very much, partly because Hunter was not in sympathy with the attempts to depolarize the campus. More importantly, however, the Strax demonstration took centre stage very shortly after the Memorial Hall meeting. Kent Thompson had played his part, and with the failure of his attempt to hold the centre together, he retired from the stage to watch the events of the rest of the year with bitter bemusement. He was not again to be involved in campus politics.

**

On Saturday, September 21, a second broadsheet was distributed on campus, urging students to "PLAY BOOKIE-BOOK TODAY!" and explaining, in more moderate language, "WHY WE SHOULD CHUCK THE ID CARDS." The broadsheet was written by Tom Murphy, one of the radical students who had been offended by the language of the previous handout.[6] The demonstration began at 4:30 pm with Strax, Hallam and Burns once again trying to check out books without their ID cards. The head of the physics department, Allen Boone, and the dean of arts, W.S. MacNutt, the historian of New Brunswick and the Atlantic Provinces, talked to the demonstrators. MacNutt, who was also the brother-in-law of librarian Gertrude Gunn, tried to convince Hallam to

Gertrude Gunn, University Librarian

use more normal channels to make his protest. Gunn reported that MacNutt did so "with interruptions and irrelevancies from Dr. Strax who appeared reluctant to leave Hallam alone with his dean." The library closed at 5:30 pm, its scheduled closing time, but the basement study hall, due to remain open until midnight, was closed to prevent sit-ins, meetings or harassment of the commissionaire on duty. I met MacNutt at a party that evening and he was obviously moved by the idealism of Hallam, yet frustrated by his insistence on the necessity for the demonstration.

On Monday, September 23, the demonstration began shortly after 9:00 pm and 268 books were brought to the circulation desk before the library was closed at 10:00 pm, one hour earlier than usual. Many students, especially graduate students, were "indignant that the library's operation had again been interrupted by the protestors."[7]

The September 24, 1968 Brunswickan *reported on the library confrontation.*

Roberta Weiner's husband, Theo, was associate professor of physics. A victim of political persecution in Europe in the 1920s and 1930s who had fled Europe for Shanghai before moving to North America, Theo was particularly upset both by his wife's discomfiture and by his memories of political hooliganism which the demonstration of his departmental colleague evoked. Theo stationed himself at the library for the day to give help and moral support to his wife at the circulation desk.

Norman Strax had been asked to stop his demonstration and pursue the matter through "normal" channels. He had refused and continued to disrupt the operation of the library. The university and the library were not prepared to relinquish their authority in the matter of the ID cards in order to defuse the demonstration. Rather, it was felt that something had to be done to control Strax, who was obviously bent on a collision course with the university.

On Tuesday, September 24, Mackay suspended Strax. The president had received a report from the librarian and had met with the academic and administrative vice-presidents and with the deans of arts and science.[8] Under the *University Act*, the president was empowered to suspend any faculty member for cause on condition that he report his action and the reasons for taking it to the next meeting of the Board of Governors. Only the board could determine the fate of the faculty member. Strax was called out of his class by head of physics, Allen Boone, to be presented with a letter from the president. This letter informed him that, "effective immediately, you are suspended from the University of New Brunswick. Such suspension means you no longer have any duties to perform here, and that all rights and privileges are withdrawn which normally belong to a member of its faculty."[9] A special meeting of the Board of Governors was called for the following Saturday, September 28.

It was expected that Norman Strax, being suspended, would leave the campus and that this would bring the library demonstrations and other forms of protest to an end. Strax, however, did not leave campus but went to his office, room 130 of Loring Bailey Hall, the biology building, and moved in. This occupation had been suggested by Tom Murphy, and many students joined Strax in his office to show their solidarity with him. The office was soon christened "Liberation 130," and for almost two months it became the visible manifestation of the student revolution on campus.[10]

This was the beginning of the "Strax Affair," which consumed the University of New Brunswick for the 1968–69 academic year and was a formative influence on the development and culture of UNB in the latter years of the twentieth century. In many ways, the Strax Affair at UNB serves as a case study of one of the university crises that arose in Canada in the late 1960s. It can be compared to the conflicts at Simon Fraser University resulting from the innovations of the Department of Politics, Sociology and Anthropology;[11] to the radicalism of the Students for a Democratic University under the leadership of Stanley Grey at McGill;[12] to the issue of racism at Sir George Williams University that led to the destruction of the computer centre in February 1969;[13] and to the struggles at a variety of universities — from the University of Toronto to the University of Saskatchewan and to Dalhousie University — over student representation in university governance.[14]

Chapter 2
A UNIVERSITY FOR THE TWENTIETH CENTURY

The Strax Affair marked the end of a long period of growth and development at the University of New Brunswick under the leadership of its young and dynamic president, Colin Bridges Mackay, one of the great university builders of twentieth-century Canada. This period of expansion at UNB paralleled similar developments at other Canadian universities in the 1960s. It led to the formation of the institutional structures of Canadian post-secondary education, such as the Association of Universities and Colleges of Canada (AUCC), which linked the university presidents, and the Canadian Association of University Teachers (CAUT), the professional organization of the teaching faculty. At UNB, it was the evolving nature of the university, coupled with institutional changes in higher education and Mackay's role as a benevolent autocrat in his prime, that created the conditions for the eruption of the Strax Affair in the 1968–69 school year.

Mackay was appointed president of UNB in the spring of 1953 at the age of 32, becoming at that time the youngest president in Canadian educational history. In 1953 UNB was a medium-sized university by Canadian standards with 767 students, seventy faculty members and sixteen administrative officers, housed in nine permanent buildings on the hillside campus in Fredericton, and a separate law school in Saint John. Two-thirds of the student body came from New Brunswick and the rest were from Atlantic Canada, Quebec and Ontario, with a handful of international students. Compared with other schools at the time, UNB inclined toward the applied sciences. Engineers made up half the student body, and when added to students in forestry and in the Faculty of Science, accounted for 70 per cent of the students. Only 17 per cent of the student body was registered in the Faculty of Arts.

Mackay had been born into the New Brunswick and the UNB establishment on July 26, 1920. His father, Colin, was a respected lumber merchant, and his mother, Jeanette, was the daughter of H.S. Bridges, professor of classics at UNB. She had actually been born in UNB's Old Arts Building, now known as Sir Howard Douglas Hall. One observer claimed that Mackay was in a constant personal war between his intellectual mother and his mercantile father.

Gordon Fairweather, a long-time friend of Mackay, characterized Mackay's father as "an older man, calm, very gentle, everything the son wasn't."[1] Attorney-General of New Brunswick in the 1950s, Fairweather served as Member of Parliament for Fundy-Royal from 1962 to 1977 before being appointed first commissioner of the Canadian Human Rights Commission in 1977. Hugh Mackay, Colin's uncle, was an influential stockbroker in Saint John and also served for a period of time as the leader of the provincial Conservative party. Colin remained very close to Hugh's widow, the daughter of Sir Douglas Hazen, who had been a member of the federal cabinet under Sir Robert Borden and was later Chief Justice of New Brunswick.[2]

Born and raised in Rothesay, Mackay attended Rothesay Collegiate School and then UNB, where he completed a bachelor of arts in history in 1942. After graduation, he joined the Royal Canadian Navy and served in the Far East before commanding a landing craft on the beaches of Normandy during the 1944 invasion of Europe. Gordon Fairweather tells of a man who had served on the landing craft and described Mackay as "absolutely wild" on that occasion, concluding that it had been "mostly nerves." Fairweather felt that Mackay had run the craft the way he drove his car. "There were times," Fairweather commented, "when, driving with him, I've been as frightened as anything in my life."[3]

After the war, Mackay attended Harvard Law School but soon transferred to the University of British Columbia, where he completed his law degree in 1949. In Vancouver, he renewed his acquaintance with Norman "Larry" MacKenzie, president of UBC from 1944 to 1962, who had been president of UNB when Mackay was an undergraduate during the Second World War. MacKenzie, appointed to the Senate in 1966, was an admired friend, professor and colleague who frequently served as mentor to Mackay during his presidency.[4] Mackay practiced law with the Saint John firm of Gilbert and McGloan and also did some lecturing at the UNB Law School. This was the sum total of his experience before he was "discovered" by Lord Beaverbrook. According to Susan Montague, the author of *A Pictorial History of the University of New Brunswick,* Mackay was "energetic, enthusiastic, wholly committed and with no experience whatsoever of university administration."[5]

It was Lord Beaverbrook who gave Mackay his boost into the presidency of UNB. Beaverbrook had been raised Max Aitken in Newcastle, New Brunswick (now Miramichi), before setting out to find fame and fortune in England. In England, he became the owner of the *Daily Express* and an influential media figure in British politics, serving in the cabinets of David Lloyd George in the First World War and Winston Churchill in the Second. As he

On his appointment in 1953, Colin Mackay was the youngest president in Canadian educational history.

accumulated wealth and influence, Beaverbrook never forgot his New Brunswick origins, building a residence and a gymnasium at UNB before the Second World War and displaying his continuing generosity to the university after 1945.

A search committee had already selected a candidate in 1953 to replace Albert Truman as the outgoing president of UNB when Lord Beaverbrook, then the university chancellor, suggested to New Brunswick Premier Hugh John Flemming (premier from 1952 to 1960) that Mackay should be given the presidency. The search committee was not prepared to support Mackay because of his youth and inexperience, but was told that the Flemming government was accepting Beaverbrook's suggestion and appointing Mackay anyway. When Beaverbrook learned of objections on the UNB Senate to his promotion of Mackay, he resigned the chancellorship and demonstrated his displeasure by lunching publicly in Fredericton with the president of the University of Toronto.[6] UNB should know that it was not the only university he was prepared to support.

After Mackay's appointment Beaverbrook consented to be appointed honorary life chancellor of the university by the Flemming government. Mackay got along well with his patron. In Beaverbrook, he recognized someone with the same energy level as his own and with a similar capacity for hard work. Mackay took little time off and worked constantly at being president, even taking note pads and Dictaphones with him in his car so he could jot down ideas and plans when he was stopped at traffic lights. He told me once that Beaverbrook's capacity for work at all times and in all places had been an inspiration to him.

Some members of the UNB alumni criticized Mackay's appointment, outraged because they considered it inappropriate.[7] Mackay generally received favourable support, however. In the early 1950s, there was a sense that a younger post-war generation of leaders needed to be encouraged. Gordon Fairweather

Lord Beaverbrook and Colin Mackay, the Honorary Life Chancellor and his Vice-Chancellor, 1954.

had been elected to the New Brunswick Legislative Assembly for the first time in 1952. Another contemporary was Ken Cox, an electrical engineer, who was rising rapidly in the ranks of the New Brunswick Telephone Company and would soon put his mark on telephone service in the province. Yet other contemporaries were the McCain brothers, Wallace and Harrison, soon to make their mark with McCain Foods in the field of food processing.

Within the university Mackay was well supported by talented senior members of the faculty and staff — the chemist Frank Toole, the historian Alfred G. Bailey, the literary scholar Desmond Pacey, business manager Bev Macaulay and others. "He seemed to be able to pay a lot of attention to them and they made it possible for him to settle in."[8]

Outside the university Premier Flemming supported Mackay; both men had to get used to dealing with Lord Beaverbrook. Fairweather recalled that Beaverbrook, for all his generosity, was a cruel man who frequently took extreme positions to see what reaction he could get. "Colin would almost have a relapse and Flemming too when Beaverbrook would try to throw his weight around," he said. Some of Beaverbrook's demands, however, made eminent good sense, added Fairweather, like moving the Faculty of Law from Saint John to Fredericton, where it became a school of some distinction.[9]

In his early years on the job, Mackay was helped a great deal by Beaverbrook himself, who used his connections to bring important public figures to Fredericton: British politician Lord Hailsham, American Senator John Fitzgerald Kennedy, Indian diplomat Krishna Menon, and historian A.J.P. Taylor among others. Beaverbrook was generous to UNB, creating scholarships and funding buildings and encouraging his wealthy friends to follow his lead in donating to UNB.

In the 1950s the university was small and intimate, with the student body numbering fewer than a thousand. The new young president was friendly and approachable. He was interested in students and started out by making a point of knowing the name of every student at the university. He wore jeans, rode a bicycle and a scooter around Fredericton and was a new and dynamic figure in the somewhat sleepy New Brunswick capital.

Mackay and Beaverbrook hosted John F. Kennedy in 1957 when UNB gave him an honorary degree.

Initially Mackay saw his role to be that of building the campus that UNB needed for the changing times. As Fairweather commented, "Colin would get very excited if the government of New Brunswick didn't immediately endorse all his fancy plans, and he would lick his lips and swallow and jump around to me despite the fact that I was just a backbench member of the legislative assembly. Of course, when I was Attorney General for a couple of years, I'd get it full barrel. You couldn't be in public life in New Brunswick in those days and not know that there had to be a very major change coming."[10]

At the same time, with the encouragement of people like Toole, Bailey and Pacey, Mackay was developing a vision of what he wanted the University of New Brunswick to become: not just a provincial college but a university that would be an important centre of learning and research in Canada. Over the years, he devoted himself to the task of building this university almost single-handedly.

Frank Toole, the vice-president (academic), and Mackay looked for a way to revitalize the engineering faculty. At the time,

Francis J. Toole became UNB's first Vice-President (Academic). He retired in 1967.

the faculty "had no sense of research in the academic sense; it was completely oriented to the practice of the profession at the bachelor's level." Toole spent a sabbatical year at UBC, and while there convinced chemical engineer Les Shemilt to come to UNB to organize a department of chemical engineering. Toole believed "that to do chemistry you had to have very good chemists and very good chemists are only very good on an international scale."

Les Shemilt arrived at UNB in 1960 and was impressed by Mackay. "In my view, he had many aspects of being a great president. One was that, even though he was no scholar himself, he insisted on academic strength and academic merit and tried to make UNB a player on the national and international scene. I was very happy at UNB because I tried to build a department in that sense and it wasn't there in all of the departments or faculties." Shemilt praised Mackay because he gave the faculty freedom to develop its programs but, if it didn't act, he was also prepared to move in and take the lead. "I give him strong credit on a number of fronts," said Shemilt. "He had an ability to see academic

Leslie W. Shemilt with Alfred G. Bailey, 1965.

strengths were really the prime factor in the university, and unless you could compete scholastically on an international basis, you weren't with it. The important thing was getting very strong people, and Mackay insisted on being a player in the national university game. The only way to do that was to look beyond your own campus bounds and to be prepared to compete. In the sense of playing on the right academic ground, I think he was a very good leader. Better than most, I think."

Shemilt admired Dean of Engineering Jim Dineen, but felt that he was too generous in promoting individuals without a sufficiently strong research record. This made it difficult to hire top scholars for the chemical engineering department. At the same time, Toole and Mackay wanted to start a department of surveying engineering, and for this they hired the Czech, Gottfried Konecny directly from his home country.

"In those days," remembered Shemilt, "if you were going to

do a branch of engineering, you had to do it at the masters and doctoral levels. In other words, you had to have a research component. I knew because of Frank Toole's own concerns that I would have no difficulty with support from him in that regard. So I went with that judgement and immediately planned to build a department that could compete reasonably well across the country. Konecny did too, so for the first time we brought a more significant research component to the faculty. Dineen also revived the Department of Electrical Engineering. There were elements of research in the engineering faculty, but the general ethos was not and they were trying to change that." The first PhD in chemical engineering was awarded in 1967.[11]

Mackay's management style was autocratic — "personal, hands on and non-consultative." SRC President David Cox described him as a "control freak," while Alwyn Berland, Executive Secretary of the CAUT, who didn't like the man, felt he was "too patrician and too accepting of the idea that the chief administrative officer at the university should be able to do whatever he wanted to do." Marxist student Dan Weston felt that Mackay was "the ruling class representative, and he did his part rather well." John Oliver, editor of the student newspaper, the *Brunswickan* in 1968, thought "Colin was used to being in charge and having nobody question his authority." With all decisions having to cross his desk, some issues were not addressed in a timely fashion, and Mackay frequently procrastinated on difficult issues. He was also noted for having a temper when he became frustrated.[12]

My work as his executive assistant gave me an insight into his style and his treatment of some of the closest collaborators in his office, where both his temper and his sense of humour were frequently on display behind closed doors. Working inside the presidential office — UNB's "West Wing" — I came to realize how Mackay assigned personalized roles to some of those around him and frequently treated them as members of his extended

James O. Dineen, Dean of Engineering.

family. His secretary, "Byng" McKay, was assigned the role of the nagging mother or aunt. It was her job to keep him on schedule and to see that he took his medication. When she would remind him of his responsibilities, he would respond in a petulant tone, like a young boy who had just been reprimanded. Business Manager Chester Mahan, on the other hand, was cast in the role of the ne'er-do-well uncle who could never do things to Mackay's satisfaction. Mackay seemed to save his outbursts of temper for Mahan, frequently throwing his memos on the floor and generally bullying him in the office. I admired Mahan for rarely losing his composure in spite of the harassment he was subjected to by his president. Another identifiable member of this inner "family" was Alan Pacey, the director of information. A young man at the beginning of his career, Pacey was viewed by Mackay as the younger brother with promise, who deserved to be guided and mentored and at times to be reprimanded and otherwise bullied for his own good. Mackay's former history professor, Alfred G. Bailey, Canadian poet and ethnohistorian, who succeeded Frank

Toole as vice-president (academic) in 1967, was deferred to as a much beloved and respected uncle, whose advice was frequently accepted.

My role in that inner circle was that of a visiting cousin, especially since Bailey had convinced Mackay to hire me as his assistant in the first place. I was always treated with respect and courtesy by Mackay, although, at the same time, I was never given very much to do. It did give me a chance to listen to Mackay's end of some telephone conversations, however, and to be an audience for his quips as he hung up. After one phone call, when he had been bullying and haranguing somebody on the other end of the line, he hung up and said, "I'd hate to work for me." Another time, after receiving a report on a disruptive tactic by Strax, Mackay commented: "I'll bet Jesus Christ was a bastard too!"

***

In the 1960s, UNB embarked on a major growth spurt, with an increased demand for university education and a new willingness of governments to fund both students and universities. Across Canada the children of the post-war baby boom, who had been born in 1945 and later, reached the age of eighteen, and from 1963 started entering the universities.[13]

In the New Brunswick provincial election of 1960, the Liberal party under Louis J. Robichaud defeated Flemming's Progressive Conservative government and was faced with a number of important issues related to post-secondary education. Robichaud remained as premier until defeated by Richard Hatfield's Progressive Conservatives in the election of 1970. During the early 1960s, there was pressure from the Saint John Board of Trade for the creation of a branch campus of UNB, if not a separate university, in the city of Saint John, both to create more university places and to fulfill aspirations of civic pride.

W.C. Desmond Pacey, Dean of Graduate Studies.

At the same time, the Acadian population of New Brunswick was looking for its own university. In 1961 Robichaud created a one-man commission, headed by the economist John J. Deutsch, the administrative vice-principal of Queen's University, to study the proliferation of universities and colleges in New Brunswick. Deutsch later became the first chair of the Economic Council of Canada, and subsequently the principal of Queen's from 1968 to 1974. In 1962, the Deutsch Commission echoed the call for the creation of a branch campus of UNB in Saint John. It also recommended the relocation of St. Thomas University from Chatham to Fredericton, to share resources with UNB, and the creation of the francophone Université de Moncton, incorporating classical colleges in Moncton, Edmundston, Bathurst and Shippagan. This rationalization of New Brunswick higher education was enacted in 1964.[14]

As more students were looking for university places, an increasing amount of government money was available to assist their participation in post-secondary education. During the

1950s, only $30,000 had been available annually for student loans, jointly funded by the federal and provincial governments. With the introduction of the *Canada Student Loans Act* in July 1964, the federal government took over the New Brunswick student loan program, increasing both the number of loans granted and the average amount of each loan. By 1968 more than $5.5 million was available annually to New Brunswick students for loans and bursaries.

By 1968 UNB was a very different university in both size and composition than it had been fifteen years before. The student population had increased five-fold to 4,800, and the university had changed from being a professional school emphasizing science and applied science to offering a more general education with emphasis on the humanities and the social sciences. The 1960s saw a great increase in the number of students studying in the arts faculty and a decline in the relative numbers in engineering, science and forestry. From being directly oriented to serving the professional requirements of the provincial and national economies, UNB had defined a broader educational role for itself, with an expanded commitment to education as a process of questioning and understanding the nature of society.[15]

This increased number of students required more faculty to teach them and a larger physical plant to house them. The teaching faculty expanded five-fold from 1953 to 1968. Between 1965 and 1969, an average of thirty-three new faculty members was hired each year, with over half of the new appointments being made in the Faculty of Arts. During the same period, the physical plant had increased from nine to thirty-one buildings on the Fredericton campus, along with new buildings for St. Thomas University and buildings for the branch campus in Saint John.

While the student body and the teaching faculty grew and altered over the period under review, it is striking that the university administration remained compact and relatively constant, having only increased by six from the original sixteen administrators of 1953.[16] This was largely a result of the management style of Colin Mackay. As long as the university remained small, the president retained his ability to supervise the entire operation. As it increased in size and complexity by the mid-1960s, however, Mackay and the administration were less able to control and deal with the myriad issues that arose, with the result that pressures grew from the faculty and the student body for a greater say in the operation and direction of the institution. Much of the pressure from the faculty association and from the student body in 1968–69 was directed toward a clearer definition of administrative procedures and functions. They wanted the administration to become more bureaucratic and less casual and "clubby."

Mackay was the driver in this period of growth as he found the resources to hire the faculty and to build the buildings. He went after funds from the federal and provincial governments and conducted extensive fundraising in the private sector. But the needs were great, and he never seemed to have enough money. By the late 1960s, Mackay faced new challenges when the rapid growth of UNB outstripped the willingness and ability of the province to fund the university. Mackay believed these expenditures were essential if UNB was to develop as he intended, and confident in his ability to eventually raise the funds, he presented the university with a series of deficit budgets. As Mackay put the issue to John Braddock, the managing editor of the *Atlantic Advocate* in April 1968, "Does the government want UNB to become a 'proper' university? Or does it want UNB to abandon all professional work and revert to being a college of Arts and Sciences as first established in 1785?"[17]

In response to these problems, the Robichaud government invited John Deutsch to return in the mid-1960s to study the issue of university financing. In his second report, Deutsch recommended the creation of a New Brunswick Higher Education

Commission as an intermediary between the universities and the government, to study the needs of the universities and to advise the government on appropriate levels of funding in higher education.[18] The first chair of the commission, appointed in 1967, was Jim O'Sullivan, a 1959 UNB graduate in business administration, and former secretary to the two Deutsch Commissions. O'Sullivan was given the unenviable task of belling the cat, placed as he was between Mackay's ambitious and unrestricted deficit financing and the finite coffers of the Province of New Brunswick.

***

UNB's pattern of growth was repeated at other Canadian universities as they expanded in the 1950s and 1960s. This expansion led to greater concerns on the part of faculty about terms and conditions of employment, about procedures for promotion and tenure, about the protection of academic freedom and about participation in university governance. Until the Second World War, the Canadian professoriate had been little concerned about issues of academic freedom and tenure and had been quite willing to leave the defence of academic freedom to university presidents who were coming under pressure from government and business to control the teaching, publications and public utterances of faculty members. While the American Association of University Professors (AAUP) had been founded in 1915 to protect academic freedom and tenure in American universities, little need was felt for a similar organization in Canada until 1951, when the Canadian Association of University Teachers (CAUT) was founded, based on the American model.

In its early years, in addition to encouraging the formation of local faculty associations, such as the Association of University of New Brunswick Teachers (AUNBT) in 1956, the CAUT took up issues of faculty salary and benefits as it sought to establish co-operation

Portrait of Colin B. Mackay by Karsh of Ottawa.

between these various associations. It was the Harry Crowe Affair at Winnipeg's United College[19] in 1958–59, however, that first brought the CAUT into prominence as a defender of faculty rights and academic freedom. When the principal of United College tried to fire historian Harry Crowe for writing a private letter that was critical of the college and its administration, Crowe turned to the CAUT for support. The Crowe Affair and the CAUT involvement became a *cause célèbre* as the first major case of academic freedom to be investigated by the CAUT. The Crowe Affair established the reputation of the CAUT, and as a result the association established a permanent national office in Ottawa and created a standing committee on academic freedom and tenure. Up to this time, hirings and firings in Canadian universities had been pretty much a matter of arbitrary decision-making. The CAUT, in the 1960s, sought to define appropriate and fair procedures for hiring, firing and granting of tenure, which they sought to have endorsed by Canadian universities. The CAUT was pushing for change and leading the country in defining these issues.[20]

In 1967, the CAUT published its "Policy Statement on Academic Appointments and Tenure." This document was described by political scientist David Cameron as "a bold, pre-emptive step in the definition of tenure in Canada."[21] While it was not officially accepted by the AUCC, which represented the university presidents, the statement was used as the basis for discussions between individual faculty associations and university administrations as the issue of tenure and procedures for the dismissal of faculty came to be defined in subsequent years.[22] It set out the basis on which the CAUT was going to judge matters that were brought to its attention, and it became the basis for the CAUT intervention in the Strax Affair.

Issues of university governance also became critical in the 1960s. In 1962, the CAUT and the AUCC, with support from the Ford Foundation, co-sponsored a study of faculty participation in university governance. Sir James Duff of England's Durham University and Robert O. Berdahl of San Francisco State University were named as the two-man Duff-Berdahl Commission, which submitted its report in 1964. The report recommended reform of university governments across Canada to give faculty members a much greater say in the running of the universities, through faculty dominance of academic senates and direct faculty representation on boards of governors. The commission also recommended that faculty participate in the selection of senior university administrators who should serve for limited terms of office.[23] The Duff-Berdahl Report was a call to universities to make fundamental revisions to their operating policies to recognize a new role for the professoriate.[24]

Under Mackay's leadership, UNB set about designing a university structure where the faculty would have the controlling voice in internal matters. Before 1968, the university was governed by a senate and a university council. The Senate was composed of senior administrators and members of the general public, many appointed by the Lieutenant-Governor-in-Council. The University Council was composed of senior administrators, faculty deans and elected members of the faculty, although the academic administrators tended to outnumber the elected faculty. Both governing bodies were chaired by President Mackay.

An internal University Committee with majority representation from the faculty was charged with developing a new University Act. Doug Pullman, the founding head of the sociology department, recognized the significance of the moment, believing this to be "the most important committee to be formed in the history of the university." The committee held its first meeting on March 11, 1967, and within two months had achieved consensus on the future shape of the government of UNB.[25] The committee agreed on a Board of Governors to replace the existing Senate and a Senate to replace the University Council, with the president to chair both bodies. Considering the role of the Board of Governors in providing oversight and guidance to the work of the president as chief executive officer, this was an unfortunate decision but, given the dominant role and personality of Mackay, it was an understandable outcome. The committee accepted the principle of faculty and student representation on the board: four faculty members were to be elected to the board, while the students were to be represented by a non-student rector. The number of elected faculty members was always to be a majority on the Senate, which was intended to have full control of academic matters in the university. Students were to be represented on senate committees, but not initially on the Senate.[26]

In the development of UNB, 1968 was a pivotal year. The University Committee recommended to the Senate, with the concurrence of President Mackay, that the principles enunciated by the Duff-Berdahl Report be adopted and implemented at UNB, thereby giving the teaching faculty significant representation on a future Board of Governors and dominance on a future Senate. The *UNB Act* of 1968 in effect democratized the university. The teaching faculty would now be in a position to engage the administrative officers of the university, some representative students and representatives of the outside community in a process of collegial discussion and decision-making, as befitting the community of scholars.

Would this collegial aspiration work under Mackay's autocratic management of the institution? Could the issue of student representation be incorporated into the new constitution? And would the teaching faculty prove capable of shouldering the responsibility of collegial and democratic decision-making? Within three months of the passage of the *UNB Act*, the new constitution would be put to the test by Norman Strax, his demonstration at the Harriet Irving Library and his subsequent suspension by Colin Mackay.

Chapter 3
SOURCES OF STUDENT RADICALISM AT UNB

Student radicalism at the University of New Brunswick developed against the provincial background of radical social change and the equally strong suspicion of change felt by many New Brunswickers. While student radicalism in Canada sought to emulate the example of the American civil rights movement and the 1964 Free Speech Movement at the University of California Berkeley, its direct antecedent was the anti-nuclear movement of the 1950s, which took shape in Canada as the Combined Universities' Campaign for Nuclear Disarmament (CUCND). By the mid-1960s, the Student Union for Peace Action (SUPA) was the manifestation of the New Left in Canada but, when that movement lost its dynamic in 1967, some of its members diverted their energy and ideals to the Canadian Union of Students (CUS) and the Canadian University Press (CUP).[1]

In the 1960s the context was set for radicalism at the University of New Brunswick by the Liberal government of Louis J. Robichaud. Robichaud had studied under Father Georges-Henri Levesque in the Faculty of Social Science at Laval University in the 1940s, where he had imbibed many of the same ideas for secular social change that were to spur the Quiet Revolution of Jean Lesage in Quebec in the 1960s. Robichaud was chosen to lead the Liberal party of New Brunswick in 1958 during a period of co-operation between the premiers of the four Atlantic Provinces that forced the federal government to pay attention to the needs of the Atlantic region. This "Atlantic Revolution" had been effective in loosening the purse-strings in Ottawa, particularly after the election of the Progressive Conservatives under John Diefenbaker in 1957 and their reelection with a greater majority in 1958. By the time that Robichaud's Liberals defeated the Progressive Conservative government of Hugh John Flemming in 1960, Robichaud was well positioned to institute significant changes in the society, culture and economy of New Brunswick. As New Brunswick's first elected Acadian premier, Robichaud, in addition to having ideas and a sense of mission as a result of his studies at Laval, was also fired by his realization of the second-class status of his own Acadian people within New Brunswick. The availability of federal resources for the Atlantic region helped to make significant changes possible.

At the beginning of his administration, the report of the Deutsch Commission on higher education was particularly important to Robichaud because it recommended bringing together the francophone *collèges classiques* in Moncton, Shippagan, Bathurst and Edmundston to create the Université de Moncton. Opened in 1963, this institution gave the Acadians a university of their own with the implicit challenge to Acadian youth to advance themselves and their society educationally.[2]

Robichaud wanted to improve the lot of the poor, and especially the Acadian poor, in his province. In practical terms, his new program was spurred by specific difficulties connected with municipal finance: richer municipalities were able to provide their people with a variety of social and educational benefits, while poor municipalities were forced to live within their restricted means. In 1962 the government commissioned J. Edward Byrne, a Bathurst lawyer, to chair a five-man Royal Commission on Finance and Municipal Taxation. Completed in 1963, the commission's report recommended the centralization of the provincial taxing authority, in order to provide the people of New Brunswick with a more equitable distribution of educational and social services. The necessary legislation, which eliminated county councils, consolidated municipal services in health and education and provided for bureaucratic centralization in Fredericton, was enacted in 1966 and 1967 as the Program of Equal Opportunity. Such a massive change needed to be grounded in a well-designed bureaucratic apparatus. To achieve this, the Robichaud government recruited key senior civil servants from Saskatchewan, who had formerly worked for the CCF/NDP government of Tommy Douglas there and were thoroughly familiar with designing and managing a modern welfare state. This ensured the professionalism of the New Brunswick civil service and the long-term stability of the program.[3]

This "Robichaud Revolution" was welcomed by many, but was equally resisted by many parts of anglophone New Brunswick. Change, whether brought about by the provincial government on behalf of the Acadian community or, later, by the demands of university students, challenged those in the province who wanted to preserve existing ways, social structures and value systems.[4] Prosperous English-speaking areas in the mid-1960s saw their cherished education programs in danger of being undermined for lack of funds and their tax dollars being spent on the poorer Acadian parts of the province. Particular resentment was felt in Fredericton, where Robichaud, the Acadian upstart, became a figure of public hatred and vilification. Vicious stories about Robichaud's private life and that of his wife circulated through the living-rooms of Fredericton. The whispering campaigns were

President Mackay and Premier Louis Robichaud host Queen Mother Elizabeth at UNB, 1967.

given credence by the crusade against Equal Opportunity pursued by Michael Wardell, the right-wing publisher of Fredericton's *Daily Gleaner* and a former employee of Beaverbrook. Wardell became the self-proclaimed champion of English New Brunswick and defined the poles and the tone of public debate. This included a suggestion from Wardell that Robichaud should be horse-whipped through the streets of Fredericton. A member of the UNB psychology department, with some exaggeration, described the atmosphere of Fredericton in 1967 as akin to the hatred that pervaded Dallas in 1963 on the eve of Kennedy's assassination.

For Canadians, 1967 was the year of the Montreal World's Fair — Expo 67 — and the centennial of the 1867 Confederation. Across Canada, this was an era of good feeling. For those living in Fredericton, centennial year meant trips to see the marvels of Expo 67, subsidized tours by the Stratford Shakespearean Company and the National Ballet of Canada, student exchange visits and a variety of local projects in the name of the centennial. One of these projects was a new government office building in central Fredericton, designed to house the expanded provincial civil service under Equal Opportunity, and appropriately named the "Centennial Building." There was a revived sense of national unity, much of which was commercial and political hype, but which also represented a deeply-felt commitment to the Canadian nation that really did seem to have come together for this celebration year.[5]

If Canadians felt positively about the celebration of the centennial, and anglophone New Brunswickers were somewhat less enthusiastic about the Robichaud government, they did not feel as strongly about events in the rest of the world. The civil rights movement and the war in Vietnam were, after all, American issues, not Canadian. We might be sympathetic but felt it was really none of our business, even though the nightly television news seemed to make it everybody's business.

**

Student radicalism was a given at almost all Canadian universities in the late 1960s. Students were no longer content to be passive recipients of their education but demonstrated an increased interest in determining for themselves the nature and content of that education. In some universities, this resulted in demands for greater student involvement in university governance; in others it resulted in calls for student-initiated innovations in university education.[6]

When the 1966 Duff-Berdahl Commission recommended a greater participation by the teaching faculty in running the universities, it said little about any similar involvement for students. This posed a challenge to student leaders in Canada, and in subsequent years, students continued their demands for greater participation on the governing bodies of the universities. Historian Roberta Lexier claims that "the democratization of university campuses was the primary issue for the student movements in English Canada throughout the sixties."[7]

A number of activist students were reformist, seeking to work within existing university structures and committees, while other students tended to be more radical, seeking to use student power to challenge university administrations, and if necessary, to force a violent confrontation. The syndicalist *Union générale des étudiants de Québec* (UGEQ) had been formed as a strong inter-university union to secure the demands of Quebec students through trade union-style negotiations with university administrations. The UGEQ example was picked up in English Canada at McGill and at Simon Fraser University with the creation of the syndicalist Students for a Democratic University (SDU), which became the institutional home of student radicalism on both those campuses.

In addition to student representation in governance, student activism was aroused over issues of freedom of the student press and over student involvement in radical educational innovation, including the design of their own courses and their own grading schemes. The educational experiment of Rochdale College in Toronto fit into this category. Some student movements had wider social goals. As a vehicle of Quebec nationalism, UGEQ sought to use university students to shape the future development of French Canada. At McGill, the SDU took up the call for "McGill *français*" and the admission of a much higher percentage of francophone students. At Sir George Williams University, many black students from the West Indies and their white radical supporters accused a biology professor of racism and eventually demonstrated their frustration by destroying that university's computer centre in February 1969.

Student radicals were often assisted and supported by radical faculty members, many of them junior and recently hired. With the expansion of the universities, many new faculty came to Canadian universities from graduate schools in either America or Britain, where they had themselves been involved in radical politics.

Simon Fraser University opened its doors for the first time in Burnaby, B.C. in September 1965, and from the beginning, its students sought to emulate the activism of the Free Speech Movement at Berkeley. Simon Fraser had hired a number of young and radical faculty and earned a reputation as the most radical university in Canada. The Department of Politics, Sociology and Anthropology (PSA) was designed to be interdisciplinary, experimental and innovative. In his book on Simon Fraser, Hugo Johnston claims that the PSA Department was a "bizarre and exciting place."[8] The faculty conceived of their department as a partnership between faculty and students, where students had parity with the faculty on all issues, including the granting of promotion and tenure. This did not sit well with the university administration.

Given the existence of radicalism in most Canadian universities, the way that university administrations responded to student and faculty challenges determined whether a campus would be peaceful or troubled. In many universities, such as the University of Toronto under the presidency of Claude Bissell, the presidents sought to prevent the radicals from developing a broad power base by responding to the demands of the reformist students. H. Rocke Robertson at McGill and Kenneth Strand at Simon Fraser similarly isolated the radicals by ensuring that students be given representation on the university Senates.

Some university administrations acted with determination in dealing with student demonstrations or with disruptive faculty. President Strand called the RCMP to the Simon Fraser campus to end the occupation of their administration building in the fall of 1968. Following procedural consultations with the CAUT, McGill and Simon Fraser acted to remove difficult faculty members, such as political scientist Stanley Grey at McGill and the radical faculty of Simon Fraser's PSA Department. The administration of Sir George Williams University, however, was unable to respond to the charges of racism in any way that would satisfy the radicals there who seemed bent on a course of destruction.

In some cases, university administrations were guided by external factors, as the general public grew weary and intolerant of concessions to student radicals. At times, provincial governments, such as that of Premier Ross Thatcher of Saskatchewan, threatened university administrations with takeover if they could not control their radical students.

The CAUT was another source of external pressure. It had extended its influence as the voice of the faculty throughout the decade of the 1960s, by supporting a larger role for faculty in university governance and by developing its policy on academic freedom and tenure. It had also developed the strategy of censuring those universities that failed to implement supportive policies for the faculty. In 1967 the CAUT had been invited by the Simon Fraser Faculty Association to investigate the relationship between the president and the faculty. Its report resulted in the imposition of censure on that university in May 1968 and the subsequent firing of President MacTaggart-Cowan.[9]

The original sources of student radicalism at UNB came from connections with national movements and organizations that encouraged students to question the values of their society and to advocate ever more loudly for the rights of students. The Canadian Union of Students (CUS) and the Canadian University Press (CUP) acquired advocates and supporters among the students of UNB, just as a few students at UNB were prepared to challenge American foreign policy and its Canadian supporters. The Student Christian Movement (SCM) brought a moral dimension to student radicalism. There is no evidence of any externally driven conspiracy to radicalize the students. What was noticeable was that as individual UNB students became caught up in some of the larger issues of the day, they made them their own and became active in promoting and encouraging changes in more radical directions.

***

Lawson Hunter, a student from Florenceville, New Brunswick, was in the final year of a science program when he was elected president of UNB's Student's Representative Council for the 1966–67 school year. As such, he was an active participant in the debates of the CUS of that year, as its leadership was becoming progressively more radical and as the Canadian student movement was splitting into left and right wings. Hunter, who had little sympathy for the right-wing "stick to your knitting and stuff," developed his own sense of the importance of student empowerment and student participation in university governance. Graduating in the spring of 1967, he entered the UNB Law School in the fall of 1967 on a Beaverbrook Law Scholarship. In 1967, he had been elected president of the Atlantic Association of Students, and as a result became a member of the Board of Directors of the CUS. In the summer of 1967, he was hired by the CUS to promote co-operative housing in the Maritimes.

In 1958 Howard Adelman, an undergraduate philosophy student at the University of Toronto, had been hired by its Campus Co-operative to develop co-op housing at the university. On his advice, the co-op bought up a number of residential properties and turned them into student residences and eventually formed a non-profit company, Co-operative College Residences, Inc. Adelman encouraged the federal government to change the regulations of the Central Mortgage and Housing Corporation to finance 95 per cent of co-op housing on the basis of a 5 per cent equity investment, which made co-op student housing fiscally feasible in the 1960s. As a junior faculty member at York University in the late 1960s, Adelman was one of the builders

Lawson Hunter.

of the experimental "free university" of Rochdale College in Toronto, which opened in the fall of 1968.

The New Brunswick Residence Co-op was founded during Hunter's term as SRC President in 1966–67. He knew Adelman well and had emulated his approach by buying up houses in downtown Fredericton and on the north side of the river. In the winter of 1967–68, under Hunter's leadership, the co-op became more ambitious. Inspired by Adelman and the architects connected with Rochdale, plans were drawn up for two new co-op apartment buildings in Fredericton.[10] Hunter took it upon himself to get provincial government support and to sell the idea to

Mackay by convincing him of the possibility of securing inexpensive funds for residence construction. With Mackay's assistance, he then sought the approval of the Board of Governors for the construction of these residences on campus.

In spite of his work for residence co-ops, Hunter didn't live in them. He was a proctor in MacKenzie House men's residence from 1967 to 1969 and continued his regional work for the CUS. At the same time, being personable, intelligent and articulate, he became an influential senior statesman among the students, many of whom looked to him for practical advice and political guidance.[11]

Lawson Hunter was at the centre of the on-campus radicalism of 1968-69 and was an important link with radical developments in the Canadian student community. He was a tactical and strategic thinker and was not averse to advising protestors and demonstrators if they sought his advice. And yet he was not an obvious participant, being conscious of his goal to establish co-op housing on campus and being aware of what was expected of him as a law student and also as a residence proctor. Thus, he always had a neat haircut and dressed conservatively, often with tie and sports jacket, and he rarely participated in any public demonstrations. While sympathetic to the protestors in Liberation 130, he never participated in their sit-in.

***

Tom Murphy was another prominent radical. He came to his radicalism through the values of the social gospel as advocated by the Student Christian Movement (SCM) at UNB. Murphy could best be described as an ethical activist who was not prepared to look the other way and keep quiet when he saw a wrong being committed. Because of this, he frequently provided articulate leadership in organizing protest within the student community.

I first met Tom Murphy in 1961 as an enthusiastic thirteen-year-old who had just joined the Cathedral Scout Troop in Fredericton, of which I was the scoutmaster. At Fredericton High School, Murphy had considered himself a supporter of the Progressive Conservative party of Prime Minister John Diefenbaker and had even waved flags at a rally for Diefenbaker in Saint John. After enrolling in UNB's Faculty of Arts in 1965, Murphy became involved with the SCM under the guidance of its general secretary, George Mossman. Murphy claims that the SCM was primarily responsible for his radicalism in the latter 1960s: "I realized very quickly that the SCM was not simply about pious Christianity but was about social change and social justice and that the game plan for the SCM was to do a lot of things on campus that would try to create a context for understanding a broader range of ideas."[12]

The SCM was one of the original radical organizations at UNB, as it was in the rest of Canada. George Mossman was an ordained United Church minister from Summerside, PEI, who had a breadth of background, having studied in Germany and in Britain. He was very much a social activist and proved adept at encouraging students to become socially aware and active in bringing about change. He was a subtle revolutionary and not an obvious one. Quiet and somewhat diffident in manner, and at times awkward and self-conscious, Mossman worked through personal contacts and did not give the SCM the appearance of an influential radical organization in the 1960s.[13] Les Shemilt, who chaired the SCM faculty advisory council, and whose son was an active member of the SCM, believed that Mossman was "enough of a scholar himself that he could see the necessity of the SCM always purporting to try to stand for critical discussion and examination. One of the things that Mossman was able to do with students was give them ideas and then get them to take over and run with the ball."[14] Under Mossman's leadership, the SCM brought intellectually challenging speakers to the campus, organized study groups and conferences on specific issues and sent students to conferences and meetings

Tom Murphy, 1968.

all over Canada and the United States.[15]

The SCM was guided and financed in the mid-1960s by an advisory council made up of members of the UNB faculty and former members of the SCM, which sought funding from the university and from local churches. Because the advisory council had decided on Mossman as a full-time general secretary in the mid-1960s, it was always in some financial difficulty, since it had to raise funds to pay the appropriate salary for a United Church minister. The bulk of the funding for Mossman's position came from the head office of the United Church, from the Anglican Synod and from UNB, which also provided an office. At times the non-denominational nature of the SCM made it less attractive to individual churches, although the UNB branch was initially supported by the Baptists and by some Roman Catholics.

Les Shemilt had been involved with the SCM throughout his undergraduate and graduate student life and claims that he took

George Mossman, General Secretary of the Student Christian Movement.

a job at the University of British Columbia in the 1950s because President Larry MacKenzie was a strong supporter of the SCM and had been at one time its national treasurer. When Shemilt moved to UNB in 1960, he immediately joined the SCM advisory council and soon became its chair. Under George Mossman's leadership, the SCM at UNB "was one of the most active university units in the country." One of the reasons for the initial success of this branch was the strong support it received from Colin Mackay, whose mentor was Larry MacKenzie, and who "had a sense of ecumenicity and an interest in trying to get religious studies in a more formal way as part of the university curriculum."[16]

In January 1967 the UNB branch of the SCM sponsored an Atlantic regional conference entitled "Values, Change, and Action — 67," designed "to evaluate proposals for action and work out student roles in a changing society." The featured keynote speaker was Saul Alinsky, the executive director of the

Industrial Areas Foundation from Chicago. Billed as a "tough-minded champion of 'participatory democracy,'" and as the "author of *Reveille for Radicals* (written in prison)," Alinsky was a noted community organizer and agent for change, who spoke at the well-attended conference of his experiences in organizing poor communities to mobilize themselves to effect radical social change.[17] Some years later, when Barack Obama became a community organizer in Chicago, before his entry into national politics, it was Alinsky's methods and processes that he was following.[18] This conference helped generate an awareness of the importance of radical social change among those from Fredericton who participated, and many of the on-campus radicals later quoted chapter and verse from Alinsky's manuals in developing their tactics.

The 1967 conference was followed by a series of well-attended, SCM-organized teach-ins during the 1967–68 and 1968–69 school years, dealing with such topics as "The Morality of Violence in the Vietnam War," "The Role of the Student in the University," "Sexuality," "Christianity and Revolution: Paradox or Promise?" and in October 1968 First Nations activist Kahn-Tineta Horn spoke on "The Indian Situation in North America."

John Oliver, who became the editor of the student newspaper, the *Brunswickan*, in the spring of 1968, had been invited by George Mossman to attend an SCM conference in Cleveland at Christmas 1967 as part of a UNB delegation, even though he had not been a member of the SCM. Oliver remembers being impressed by seeing people burn their draft cards at this conference and developed there his belief that American behaviour in Vietnam was unreasonable.[19] "In terms of developing awareness on campus and encouraging the emergence of radical politics," claimed Tom Murphy, "the SCM was very much in the forefront."[20] Lawson Hunter, on the other hand, did not feel that the SCM at UNB was either broadly based or in the mainstream of

Mackay with his presidential predecessors in 1963. Left to right: Milton F. Gregg, Albert Truman, Colin B. Mackay, Norman A. M. Mackenzie.

the student movement. He felt it was largely George Mossman and a few students.[21]

The *Brunswickan* was another source of radicalism at UNB, through its links with other campus papers through the Canadian University Press (CUP). Tom Murphy, who started writing a column for the paper in 1967, felt that the *Brunswickan* "wasn't just the student campus newspaper, but was a real collective of its own." In December of that year, Murphy was sent to a CUP conference in Vancouver as a stand-in for editor John Oliver. In Vancouver, Murphy met the editors of the other Canadian student newspapers and realized that "the *Brunswickan* was just one of many lefty radical student links across Canada." The CUP ran a wire service emphasizing radical events on Canadian campuses, and much of that found its way into the *Brunswickan*, especially in the years prior to the Strax Affair, after which UNB students were generating radical news on their own. Identifying themselves with the student proletariat, *Brunswickan* staffers had nothing but contempt for the SRC and the student politicians, all of whom were assumed to be working to build up their resumés for future careers in the corporate world.[22]

John Oliver found that many of the people associated with the CUP were Marxist-Leninists. Frank Goldspink had been a student journalist at the University of Waterloo, and in 1968 he appeared at UNB, sent by the CUP from Winnipeg as a field worker to help produce the *Brunswickan*. Like the other people in CUP, Goldspink was also a Marxist-Leninist and knew the key figures on the Canadian radical left. Oliver got money from the SRC in the fall of 1968 to hire the knowledgeable and experienced Goldspink, who helped him to get out a paper every week, which was a challenging task for an amateur editor like Oliver.[23]

Dave Jonah entered the arts faculty at UNB in the fall of 1968. He volunteered to work for the *Brunswickan* and received his initial training from Goldspink who was "older, experienced, and worked as a real newspaperman." The newspaper that fall was an exciting place to work, he recalls. "There was a lot of drama, and the *Brunswickan* in one way or another was directly in the epicentre of everything that seemed to be going on." Jonah felt that Goldspink's role was to "bolster the backbone of the *Bruns*." He was very much a tactician of the student revolution and was often dispensing tactical advice to the *Brunswickan* staff. Jonah commented that "to an awful lot of people, the *Bruns* appeared to be the spiritual home, the theological centre. You'd come in for your little fix and go back out to write your report."[24]

***

This was the University of New Brunswick that welcomed Norman Strax when he became a member of the physics department, bringing his experience of American radicalism and the movement against the war in Vietnam. He did not so much introduce radicalism to the Fredericton campus as serve as a catalyst for the radical potential that already existed. According to David Cox, "Strax happened to be the lightning rod for circumstances that would have boiled over anyway; he was the guy that was the focal point."[25]

Before leaving the United States, Strax had been involved in the antiwar movement. As he told it, he had been politicized when he was at Harvard. Having never been involved in protest before, he decided to join an anti-war march to Boston Common to find out what it was all about. En route, the march was heckled by some motorcyclists, who even lunged at the marchers and knocked one person over. When Strax protested to a nearby policeman that the marchers were peaceful and did not deserve this, the policeman hit him on the head and shoulder with his billy club, and according to Strax, that was his epiphany as a radical.[26]

Norman Strax was born in Brooklyn in 1935 and raised in New York City and on Long Island. He was one of six children of the radiologist Philip Strax, a pioneer in the use of mammography in the detection of breast cancer. Norman majored in physics at Princeton, graduating in 1957, then moved to Harvard for graduate study, earning his doctorate in 1966.[27]

With a freshly minted doctorate, he was hired to teach at UNB in July 1966, one of many faculty members hired to meet the needs of the expanding university that year. At the age of thirty-one, he was appointed to a probationary position as assistant professor of physics for a vague term "of from one to two years." He made a good initial impression, and in November of that year, Allen Boone, head of the physics department, wrote to the president that Strax was "keenly interested in his students and his teaching" and that he was "doing a fine job."[28]

Strax was a great admirer of the nineteenth-century radical author and philosopher Henry David Thoreau, and by moving to New Brunswick, Strax felt that he had discovered his own Walden

Norman Strax, September 1968.

Pond, as described by Thoreau, in an area unspoiled by urban sophistication. Strax lived the pastoral life in a house in the country north of Fredericton, on the Royal Road to Stanley. He settled there and commuted to the campus in his Volkswagen beetle. An animal lover, it was said that he soon had a houseful of cats.

When Strax arrived at UNB, he realized how non-political and uninvolved most Canadian students were, and he set out to raise their consciousness of issues in the world around them. In early 1967, a group of individuals came together to demonstrate their opposition to the war in Vietnam. Strax was a leading figure in the group, which called itself the "Mobilization Against the War in Vietnam." He was joined by like-minded students, one of whom was Tom Murphy. The main purpose of the "Mobilization," as it came to be known, was to sensitize the relatively insensitive UNB students to the issues of war and peace, exploitation, inhumanity, community and brotherhood that had become vital forces on American campuses and in the international student community. Initially, it set up literature tables in the Student Centre, printed its own newsletter, sought to enlist members and later, sponsored speakers and films.

There was a degree of intensity and commitment in the Mobilization that set it apart from most of the other campus student groups. Murphy recalled that the Mobilization would set up its book display on Wednesdays or Thursdays in the Student Centre and that before the day was over some other students — engineers, foresters or nurses — would come by to call them pinkos and communists, to harass them and to knock their display table over. Early student supporters of the Mobilization included Dan Weston, Clayton Burns, John Oliver and Bronwyn McIntyre. While there were other women involved, Murphy felt that McIntyre was the only one who was actively involved in her own right in this pre-feminist era, having taken a principled stand after studying the issues involved.[29] Strax and his followers became the centre of anti-war protest on campus in 1966–67.

The "Mobilization Against the War in Vietnam" occasionally referred to itself as the "SDS Mobilization," which raises the question of whether it was a chapter of the American Students for a Democratic Society, the group behind many of the campus protests and anti-war demonstrations in the United States. It appears that the SDS designation was used by the Mobilization primarily for propaganda effect. According to Tom Murphy, there were no structures, elected positions, memberships or membership lists in the Mobilization. "To say you were a member of Mobilization or not," said Murphy, "was just simply to use something to self-identify."[30]

Franz Martin of Locke Mills, Maine came to UNB in the fall of 1968 from the University of Maine at Orono. A third-year student, he was selected as one of the first to participate in a new student exchange program between the University of Maine and the University of New Brunswick. In Orono, he had joined the Maine chapter of the SDS by helping out with a demonstration against a visit by Vice-President Hubert Humphrey. According to Martin, the SDS organization in Orono was as loose as it was in Fredericton, but he did have the option of taking out a membership in the umbrella SDS organization. He did this for the first time after he came to UNB and then worried because he had sent his membership dues to the SDS Chicago office in Canadian dollars. He recently recalled that "there was no organizational link between the radicals at UNB and the larger Chicago-based SDS," and that "Strax's approach to organizing was much too anarchistic to have fit into anyone else's political framework." Certainly, when some members of the Maine SDS visited Fredericton, "they did not like Strax, saw no future in what we were doing and never made any further contact."[31]

A shy man, Strax was soft-spoken, gentle and kind, idealistic and otherworldly. He struck a number of people as being naïve, rather inexperienced and somewhat inarticulate, although he was able to express himself strongly on topics of concern to him. One observer, a student at the time, felt that he was one of those unusual professors who are genuinely interested in their students, while others commented that he was a genuinely nice man, "a very, very nice man." In appearance, some found him to be "interesting looking," while others found him to be unattractive, as he was usually unkempt and somewhat dirty and "had the weakest handshake imaginable."[32]

Fredericton and UNB were not a comfortable fit for Strax, since in many ways, he was seen as an outsider in the smug conservatism of the Fredericton community. He was an American, he was a radical and he was Jewish, all of which would set him apart from the mainstream. And yet, since he had deliberately rejected the values of the American community from which he had come, he could also feel that he was bringing new perspectives and new values to his adopted country.

As the don of MacKenzie House, I was in a position to know a broad cross-section of the faculty. Yet, when Norman Strax's name surfaced as the organizer of a trip to Washington, none of my friends or acquaintances had met the man, and no one knew very much about him. The first time I saw him was when I passed a man on the stairs leading to the third-floor Faculty Club in the Old Arts Building, wearing a jacket festooned with buttons and badges. "That," I was informed by my companion, "is Norman Strax." Strax's outfit in itself was inappropriate dress for the Faculty Club in those days.

MacKenzie House ran a weekly speaker's program that year, where a different guest was invited to the House each week to speak about some current topic. Norman Strax was invited one night to talk about the Vietnam War. To welcome him, students unearthed tin helmets and swastika arm-bands and he was confronted with a decidedly unreceptive audience. Strax gave a virtuoso performance. Speaking softly and reasonably, he brought that roomful of students around to his perspective on the war so that, by the end of the session, the tin hats were being pushed under their wearers' chairs and the armbands were ashamedly being stuffed into their owners' pockets, especially after Strax had pointed out that he was Jewish.

By the fall of 1967, Strax and the Mobilization felt that more effort was needed to raise awareness of the Vietnam War at UNB. "Stop the Draft Week" was planned as a major international demonstration against the war in Vietnam in late October 1967, culminating in a march on the Pentagon on October 21. The organizers expected to bring thousands of protestors to Washington for this event, representing students, faculty, scientists, clergy, veterans, pacifists, black people's organizations and women's organizations. Promised speakers at the demonstration included Dr. Benjamin Spock of the Committee for a Sane Nuclear Policy, Dagmar Wilson of Women Strike for Peace, and the Reverend James Bevel of the Southern Christian Leadership Conference. Featured performers included entertainers Peter, Paul and Mary and Phil Ochs. Train- and bus-loads of demonstrators were to converge on Washington from all over the United States and Canada. Supporting protests were planned for France, Sweden, Germany, Belgium, Italy, Denmark, Scotland and Norway, with particularly large demonstrations planned for England, Australia and Japan.[33]

Strax and the Mobilization wanted New Brunswick to be part of this demonstration and thus they offered return bus tickets to students and faculty for the cut rate of nine dollars for a weekend in Washington. By October 13 the Mobilization had sold 143 tickets, requiring at least three buses. Participants included faculty and students from UNB, St. Thomas University, the New Brunswick Teachers' College, UNB in Saint John, Bathurst College, Mount Allison and Acadia Universities, as well as non-university people from Fredericton. Recognizing that the ticket price and voluntary donations were unlikely to cover the cost of the buses, Strax issued a call to his university colleagues for help in meeting the anticipated deficit of $2000. He indicated that he would be willing to cover the deficit from his own funds but that, if he did so, it would interfere "with my standing policy of donating one-third of my income to peace organizations (such as SANE, CORE, SUPA, Canadian Friends Service Committee, Vietnam Summer, The Resistance, Resist, The War Resistors League, Central Committee for Conscientious Objectors, National Mobilization Committee, etc.)"[34] The buses loaded up in Fredericton on Thursday, October 19, and returned late in the evening of Sunday, October 22. Few of those who went to Washington were politicized by the experience, although many were impressed by the demonstration and were certainly more sympathetic to the Mobilization on campus afterwards.

It was the Washington trip that made Norman Strax a political figure on campus, and his action in organizing the bus trip became a matter of considerable controversy. Some faculty and other members of the provincial community were very upset that Strax had taken the students to Washington, disliking what they saw as an obvious attempt by a faculty member to preach a political doctrine to students; others were suspicious of the fact that the nine-dollar individual price for the trip did not cover all the costs and wondered what outside organization was behind Strax. Americans were also upset about these Canadians going to Washington to criticize American government policies. Maine's Senator Margaret Chase Smith likened the UNB trip to French President Charles de Gaulle's support of Quebec separatism when he visited Montreal in the summer of 1967.[35] In making a similar argument, Frances L. Churchill of Penobscot, Maine, advised Mackay that the United States and Canada were "reaping the whirlwind of permissive education — no discipline of minds or bodies — parental lack of training."[36] Mrs. Walter Cann of Brookville, NB, believed that the students "were used as dupes of the Communist parties around the world."[37]

The *King's County Record* of Sussex, NB, called for an immediate investigation by the university into the actions of the students and faculty who participated in the demonstrations in Washington. The paper was particularly upset that faculty and students would allow themselves to defy law and order and risk arrest. If the investigation "found that faculty members in particular were responsible in any way for causing this shame to New Brunswick's leading university, stern disciplinary action should be taken."[38] "A worried Mother and Dad" from Saint John wrote to Mackay that Strax "should be sent back to US and let him make his trouble there." They did not want their son, currently a UNB student, to come under his influence and were debating whether they would keep him at UNB if Strax remained.[39] In spite of this kind of pressure, Mackay held his ground, and claimed that Strax had a right to his opinions and to his activities and that it was the duty of the university to protect freedom of dissent.

The Washington trip had been a grand gesture and it gave the Mobilization more prominence on campus, but numbers did not increase much and it was still viewed as somewhat irrelevant to local concerns. It was a general student demonstration, encouraged by Colin Mackay himself in February 1968 that gave the Mobilization a new opportunity to change its tactics, both by linking with local protest and by orienting itself to more local concerns.

In early 1968 issues of university finance were of concern both to Mackay and to the students of the university. Cuts in the proposed provincial grants to the universities for 1968–69 meant that the universities would only be able to balance their budgets in the coming year by increasing student fees. The UNB SRC had previously supported universal accessibility to higher education by keeping fees as low a level as possible and had linked with the other student councils in the province to protest the government's funding decision. A march in Fredericton and a meeting with Premier Robichaud were planned to encourage the government to freeze the fees and increase the grants to the universities.

Under the leadership of SRC President Wayne Beach, UNB's council held a think-tank at the Oromocto Hotel on Saturday and Sunday, February 10 and 11, to decide what form the protest should take. Colin Mackay attended the meeting and encouraged the students in their plans to protest. He offered the students the services of the university's comptroller, Chester Mahan, to ensure they had the right figures to enable them to make a good case to the premier.

The "Freeze the Fees" demonstration took place on Tuesday, February 20. By this time, Beach's term as SRC president had expired and he had been replaced by David Cox,[40] who had been elected on February 11. In the previous year, Cox had attended a CUS conference to discuss how students should respond to government pressure to raise fees. As a result, he was well prepared to coordinate a New Brunswick-wide student demonstration on the issue. Three thousand students from across New Brunswick, led by Cox, marched on Fredericton's Centennial Building on February 20, where they received a not very sympathetic response from the premier and provincial government officials.

In setting up the march, with help and introductions from Mackay and others, Cox had arranged for the student council presidents to meet privately with Robichaud and his cabinet after the march had ended. This meeting had barely started when one of Robichaud's advisers came into the room to announce that the students had occupied the hallways of the Centennial Building and that he had had to claw his way through a mob of students to get into the cabinet room. According to Cox, as soon as this news arrived, the whole meeting fell apart.[41]

Members of the Mobilization had been on the organizing committee for the march, but from the beginning had planned to turn the march into an occupation to secure much greater publicity for their cause. When the crowd was about to disperse at the end of the march, the Mobilization took control of the demonstration. They passed out handbills declaring that the real issue was that the provincial government was under the thumb of K.C. Irving and other capitalist interests and was deliberately exploiting the workers and students of the province. They then led some of the protesting students to occupy the halls of the Centennial Building.[42]

The behaviour of the members of the Mobilization was an indication of the changing direction and tactics of that group. It was no longer American society that was corrupt but now that of New Brunswick. Local oppression and exploitation should be understood and reacted against. Mobilization members now looked for more local issues as vehicles for spreading its message to the public. The sit-in at the Centennial Building had been a good propaganda exercise, which, again, had been noticed by the provincial community. While the occupation was orderly and voluntarily brought to an end, it did demonstrate to Strax the potential for sensitizing public opinion through direct action and arguments that big government, big university and big business were undermining the rights of the average New Brunswicker.

On learning of the occupation, Cox was furious at seeing his whole strategy come apart. He left the Cabinet Room and immediately ordered the Campus Police to clear the building. "This was my red-necked engineering background coming to the fore," he later recalled. "We had not agreed on this occupation and it was not part of the deal. I'll never forget the reaction of the media, our *Brunswickan* leaders, and some of the students. At the next council meeting, a day or two later, I was hung in effigy. It was an unbelievable experience." At the council meeting, Cox was censured for calling in the Campus Police. As it turned out, they had not been very effective in clearing the building because of the number of students involved; the last students did not leave the building until much later in the day.[43]

The *King's County Record* was not impressed by the events of February 20. "The sympathy [that] orderly students may have gained was more than wiped out by the irresponsible few who parked themselves in the Centennial Building's second floor and made a mess of the place, including a University of New Brunswick professor, Dr. Norman Strax, who was among the rubbish on the second floor." When police told Strax to vacate the building, he "told them they would have to move him. He went into his worm-like limpness. Dr. Strax continued to 'serve' his university by seeking to destroy an essential student belief that they should look up to faculty members, instead of down upon them as they squirm on a floor in open defiance of the law."[44]

By encouraging the demonstration of February 20, Mackay had got rather more than he had bargained for. He quickly sent letters of apology to Premier Robichaud and Education Minister Wendell Meldrum, pointing out that, "a number of my faculty and students have begun to feel I have not been sufficiently aggressive in pursuing the cause of this University." He hoped "that no precipitous action will be taken in regard to the problems of our universities until the whole matter has been thoroughly explored by the Post-Secondary Education Commission and by the government."[45]

As protests and demonstrations exploded across the world in 1968, Norman Strax travelled to New York's Columbia University in April to participate in the demonstrations there. By August, he was with the protestors outside the Democratic National Convention in Chicago, where he was "clubbed over the head, beaten up, mishandled and physically abused" by the Chicago police as they sought to clear the protestors from the streets. As a result of his Chicago experience, Strax "grew more convinced than ever that there must be a continuous revolution against misuse of authority, non-democratic processes, and indeed the whole structure of North American society — including that in New Brunswick."[46]

If it had not been for Colin Mackay, Strax might not have returned to UNB in September 1968. Allen Boone had been much less satisfied with his performance in the second year of his appointment, and in April 1968 held a formal meeting with Strax in the presence of the dean of science, C.W. Argue. Boone told Strax that, while his teaching was reasonably good, his class attendance did "not meet the standards of this University." Nor was his research output what was expected of him. Strax had been given a lighter teaching load so that he could get on with his research, but Boone did not feel this could continue indefinitely unless Strax published some results. There was also concern about Strax's relationship with his colleagues since Boone saw "little indication of a successful and mutually profitable integration into the department."

As a result of these concerns, Boone informed Strax that he was only prepared to extend his probationary period for one more year "with the understanding that for the part of the year when travelling conditions are difficult, you will take up residence sufficiently close to the University to eliminate the missing of classes on account of the weather." Boone also wanted Strax to participate more in departmental activities, advising him that "it is unlikely these things may be accomplished without some curtailment of your present activities outside the department."[47] In spite of reminders from Boone that his letter should be considered an offer of reappointment under stipulated conditions, Strax did not reply for more than a month.[48] The assurances in his tardy letter did not satisfy Boone, however, and on May 31 he told Strax that he had "recommended to President Mackay that your association with the Department of Physics be discontinued as of June 30, 1968."[49]

Mackay, however, felt that Boone was presenting a flimsy case against Strax, which, given the nature of Strax's public activities, could easily be interpreted as the firing of Strax on political grounds. Mackay refused to accept Boone's recommendation and instead extended Strax's probationary appointment to June 30, 1969, subject to an agreement by Strax "to accept and adhere to several requirements, academic and otherwise," to be defined by Mackay and Boone.[50] On August 5, Strax accepted this extension of his probationary appointment.[51]

When Strax returned to UNB at the end of the summer, he had been pumped up by his experiences in Chicago and he knew that he had only one more year in his appointment at UNB. He was a man in a hurry and he sought out Lawson Hunter, as he occasionally did for advice and assistance. Strax wanted to know

"What we are going to do to get things moving at the beginning of the year" and mentioned to Hunter the possibility of a demonstration at the library.[52] Hunter agreed to help Strax by chairing a teach-in for students in early September when Strax could speak about his experiences at Columbia and in Chicago. Strax was also interested in making contact with young faculty members, especially those who were popular with the students. This led him to a meeting with historian Stephen Patterson in early September, which had been arranged by one of Patterson's American history students.

While his meeting with Strax didn't come to much, Patterson did, out of interest, attend Strax's presentation in September to see what he had to say. The meeting was attended by fewer than one hundred students and junior faculty and Strax spoke of his experiences in the sit-in at Columbia in April 1968. He appeared to be embarrassed when he described how the protestors had shouted at New York's finest, "Up against the wall, motherfucker!" "As he said this," Patterson recalled, "He got extremely excited about it, but he seemed very pathetic and a bit silly."[53]

Colin Mackay kept his eye on Lawson Hunter. After Hunter had appeared to show support for Strax by chairing this meeting, and before "Bookie-Book" started in the library, Mackay called Hunter into his office and warned him that his proposal for co-op residences would not receive Mackay's support in the Board of Governors if he continued to support Strax publicly. Hunter was stunned by this ultimatum, and after this meeting Mackay was very wary of him.[54] In my meetings with the president during the height of the Strax crisis, he would often ask me how my proctor was making out, frequently referring to Hunter as "Lenin." Mackay was convinced that Hunter was behind much of what was happening on campus that year and felt badly betrayed by him after he had been willing to support the construction of the new co-operative residences. The plan for the on-campus co-op residences was approved by the Board of Governors in October 1968 and it was followed by Hunter's immediate resignation as the president of the NB Residence Co-op.

Chapter 4
FROM THE CAMPUS TO THE COURTS

Norman Strax had been suspended from his duties at the University of New Brunswick on Tuesday, September 24, 1968, and all rights and privileges that normally belong to a faculty member had been withdrawn from him. One of these privileges is the use of a university office.

Strax moved into his office, Room 130 of the biology building, on Friday, September 27 and defied the president to remove him. A number of students, upset that such a mild protest in the library had elicited such a draconian response, joined Strax in the occupation and demanded that the suspension be lifted. The students had soon christened Strax's office, "Liberation 130," and it stood as a public challenge to presidential authority.

On Saturday, September 28, the Board of Governors met in special session to consider the president's action in suspending Strax. The new *UNB Act* had come into effect on July 1, and in the elections for faculty membership of the Board of Governors, law professor George McAllister, the author of the act, and historian Murray Young had been elected to three-year terms; civil engineer Eric Garland to a two-year term; and following a run-off election, chemical engineer Les Shemilt to a one-year term on the board.[1] These elected faculty members recognized their responsibility under the new act to ensure that Strax be given a fair hearing and that the board subject the president's decision to close scrutiny. They believed there must be due process and that the faculty members on the board should have a significant role in developing that process. They also saw the importance of working closely with the AUNBT.

The faculty members convinced Mackay at the board meeting to appoint an investigative committee of faculty that would meet Strax and others involved and report back to the board before any final decision was taken. This would also give the faculty members on the board time to discuss the issue with the faculty. The proposal was approved by the board and a committee was struck with board faculty members Garland and McAllister along with Doug Brewer, a popular young chemist who was the president of the AUNBT. McAllister, the New Brunswick expert on labour law, and in 1968 also the national vice-president of the CAUT, was to be the chair. The committee was instructed to determine the facts of the case and report to the board at its next meeting, scheduled for Tuesday, October 8.

The recognition of the AUNBT as a key player in this investigation represented an important step in enhancing the status of the faculty association made possible by faculty representation on the board. From its founding in 1956, the AUNBT had regarded itself as the professional association of the UNB teaching faculty. It was a loose organization that brought together all full-time faculty members — whether they were regular teaching faculty or academic administrators, such as department heads, deans or vice-presidents — to talk about terms and conditions of employment. It was affiliated with the CAUT as a constituent branch with a vote on the national council, but by

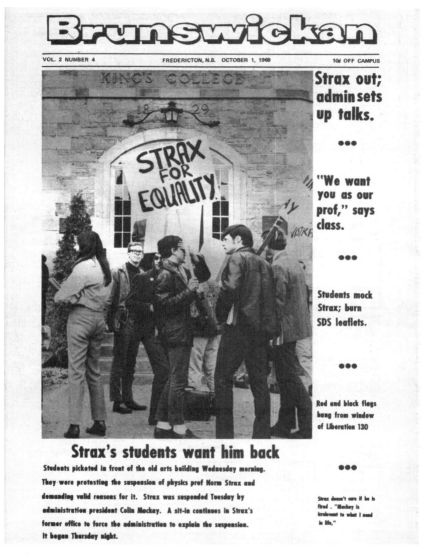

October 1, 1968 Brunswickan. *Dan Weston is the student on the right.*

and large, until the late 1960s, it looked after its own interests at UNB, serving as a lobbying agency with the president and the Board of Governors.

The AUNBT had not, however, been particularly successful in representing the faculty to the president. Mackay for years had refused to accept the AUNBT as the sole voice of the faculty and quite often preferred to select faculty members on the University Council or the Senate or other faculty members of his choosing to give advice on issues of concern to the faculty. While Mackay's behaviour was often annoying, most members of the AUNBT were loyal to the institution, respected the president with his idiosyncrasies and were willing to co-operate with him in hope that he would eventually recognize the AUNBT as the official voice of the faculty. The inclusion of the AUNBT president in the investigative committee in the fall of 1968 was, therefore, seen as an important recognition by Mackay and the board of the role of the AUNBT in the matter. By the end of the board meeting of September 28, the faculty members on the board were satisfied that they had given some useful direction and had acquired some breathing space in an increasingly polarized situation.

The Board of Governors did not, however, respond to the immediate challenge of Strax's occupation of his campus office, which was much on the mind of Colin Mackay. The faculty members on the board did not anticipate the machinations of Mackay who, in his concern to get Strax out of his office had, by the beginning of the following week, effectively invalidated the work of the McAllister Committee by taking the case out of the university and placing it before the courts. Having agreed to an investigative committee at Saturday's meeting, Mackay had gone home to Saint John for the weekend.

On Monday, acting possibly on advice from the university lawyer, Don Gilliss, Mackay had applied for an injunction against Norman Strax in the court of Justice J. Paul Barry in Saint John. Mackay first sought an interim injunction to get Strax out of his office and off the campus. This was to be followed by an injunction restraining Strax from "returning to or entering upon any

George McAllister, Professor of Law, 1974.

part of the lands and premises" of the university, as well as a declaration that Strax had been "duly and regularly suspended." The university claimed damages for "nuisance, trespass and disturbance," and called on Strax to desist from counselling students to violate the rules of the university.

When they learned of the injunction, the faculty members on the board felt they had been betrayed by the president, who had taken the matter outside the jurisdiction of the university.[2]

For the hearing on the interim injunction, Barry ordered Strax to appear before him in Saint John to explain why the injunction should not be imposed. Strax was to appear on October 1, but saw no reason why he should desert his office, his protest and his student supporters because of a court summons. With some difficulty, Lawson Hunter explained to him that failure to appear before Judge Barry would result in contempt of court charges, which were far more serious under Canadian law than under

D. Murray Young, Professor of History.

American. Reluctantly Strax acquiesced, and on October 2 and 3 he defended his position in court in Saint John with Fredericton lawyer Duff Harper as his counsel.

Economist John Earl and Harold Sharp from the School of Business Administration had looked for a lawyer who could both represent Strax and be an adviser to the demonstrating students whom they expected to suffer as a result of university retaliation. Earl had played bridge with Harper, and he and Sharp together convinced the lawyer to take on the case after unsuccessfully canvassing a number of other law firms.[3] Sharp offered to pay Harper for defending Strax, if necessary.[4] Lawson Hunter accompanied Strax to Saint John and appeared as a character witness for him, but to no effect. Barry imposed the injunction, and Strax was thereafter legally constrained from going back to the campus. He was also charged with contempt of court for his procrastination in responding to Barry's summons and was ordered to return to court in November.

In spite of the petition for the injunction, the McAllister Committee began its deliberations on Wednesday, October 2. Strax attended this meeting accompanied by his lawyers, Duff Harper and Vincent Kelly of the Ontario Bar. McAllister explained that the committee "was constituted to review and report on the circumstances of your suspension. That is the sole function of the committee and the proceedings are not in the nature of an arbitration and not in the nature of a trial." Strax and his lawyers objected that the reasons for Strax's suspension had never been stated, that the injunction blocked Strax's access to campus and that Strax had been deprived of the use of his office. They then left the meeting to convene a press conference, at which Kelly claimed that the conclusion of the committee's deliberations was predetermined. "It was a 'kangaroo court' without the procedures of natural justice." In spite of this piece of theatre, Kelly phoned McAllister the following day to ask if Strax could return to meet the committee as a voluntary witness, and when he did, he provided the committee with useful testimony in ascertaining the facts of the situation. The committee also interviewed thirteen other witnesses from the university.

In preparing its report, the McAllister Committee sought to determine to what extent the use of ID cards in the library had contributed to the crisis. While Vincent Kelly implied that Strax had been suspended because of his anti-war protest in previous years, the committee and Strax himself demonstrated that, in spite of Strax's political activism, he had been reappointed in the summer of 1968 for a further probationary year. The committee went to some length to identify the circumstances surrounding

Norman Strax leaves the courthouse followed by his lawyer, Duff Harper, October 1968.

the events in the library and was extremely careful not to express any opinions on the suspension of Strax. Its final report was submitted to the Board of Governors on November 1, 1968. In discussion with the committee, Strax had raised the question of whether his actions were really deserving of suspension, since none of the books in question were stolen or damaged and the worst imposition on the library was that it had to close early and library staff had to re-shelve the books.[5]

The results of the McAllister Committee were hardly an exercise in faculty power, and in its timidity, as a "fact-finding" exercise it failed to raise any real issues germane to the future treatment of Norman Strax. In this respect, it opened the door to CAUT intervention at UNB.

The CAUT central office had first become involved in the Strax Affair on September 30, when it was asked, presumably by faculty from UNB, if the association would be taking any position on the suspension of Strax. Following a series of hasty consultations, a meeting of the Academic Freedom and Tenure Committee was convened for October 5. It concluded that UNB's actions were indeed in violation of CAUT policy. Accordingly, the committee's chair, James B. Milner, a law professor at the University of Toronto, sent a telegram to Mackay expressing concern that Strax had not been provided with reasons for his dismissal nor had he been granted any "adjudicative procedure that would enable him to answer specific charges and debate the appropriateness of the penalty." According to Milner, UNB could either lift the suspension or provide Strax with an opportunity for arbitration. When the UNB Board took no action along either of these lines, the CAUT issued a public call for UNB to "bring the case of Professor Norman Strax to arbitration quickly."[6]

Over the years, a minority of the AUNBT membership had been impatient with Mackay's autocratic and arbitrary behaviour, had challenged him on many issues and gave their first loyalty to the CAUT in hopes that it might eventually be able to define standards for appointments, dismissals and tenure that university administrations would agree to accept. The CAUT had issued its policy statement in 1967, defining fair procedures for the establishment and protection of academic freedom and tenure, but by 1968 none of the Canadian universities had adopted this statement as official policy. The CAUT, nevertheless, acted as if it had done so and scrutinized developments at

Eric Garland, Associate Professor of Civil Engineering.

Canadian universities, and through its Committee on Academic Freedom and Tenure, reported whenever it felt that university behaviour was at variance with CAUT standards. The Strax Affair provided a perfect opportunity for the CAUT and its active supporters in the AUNBT to convince, if not force, the University of New Brunswick to adopt its policy statement.

The great set-piece event of this campus turmoil was the university's fall convocation. On Tuesday, October 8, the Board of Governors met in the board room on the second floor of the Old Arts Building. The student radicals decided to make their protest more vivid by occupying the hall outside the meeting and blocking the exit from the room. As a result, members of the board, including industrialist K.C. Irving, had to be lifted over the bodies of the radicals by security personnel in order to leave the meeting. Les Shemilt recalls that, in spite of the fact that he was in sympathy with demonstrations in support of Strax, "having my own way impeded after staggering through discussions for a couple of hours, I could feel the resentment rising in me about this and I had to screw down hard." More conservative members of the board "were quite prepared to trample on the demonstrators both literally at that stage and earlier and figuratively in the sense of the board discussion."[7] Mrs. Howard Rogers, an Alumni Board representative from Saint John, had attended the meeting in spite of the fact that her husband was ill. She worried about him, and when it came time to leave the meeting, she found that she had to step over the students, twisted her heel and was caught by two men as she was falling.[8]

In spite of the student demonstration, the October 8 board meeting did not spend a lot of time on the Strax case. In the morning, after the demonstrating students had threatened to invade the meeting, the board agreed to receive ten of them. Tom Murphy led the group and spoke about student representation on the board and about the reinstatement of Strax. Later in the meeting, the board agreed it would take no action on the Strax suspension until the report of the McAllister Committee had been made available. According to the minutes of the meeting, the board then agreed unanimously that Mackay "had taken the proper action in dealing with Dr. Strax," following his meeting with senior university officials, including "Assistant Professor Peter C. Kent, assistant to the president." It was not until I read these minutes in preparing this book that I realized that I, too, had been one of the people supposedly consulted before the suspension of Strax.[9]

I had been delegated that morning to stay close to the president's office, to protect the secretaries and to watch for

Industrialist K.C. Irving leaves the October 8, 1968 Board meeting over student protestors who are blocking his way.

a possible occupation of the office. I can remember Mackay returning from the board meeting very agitated and obviously very shaken, repeating over and over, "They're going to destroy me," and muttering, "I can't go on with this."

That afternoon, the formal opening of Ludlow Hall, the new building for the Faculty of Law, was scheduled to take place with John Turner, the federal minister of justice in the Trudeau government, in attendance. Mackay was worried about possible demonstrations, but he was saved by the dean of engineering, Jim Dineen, who rounded up a number of engineering students to "show their support for the president." The engineers marched, *en bloc*, to Ludlow Hall for the opening ceremony, arriving just in time to head off a group of radical protestors also converging on the building. The president was given loud applause and the opening ceremony went off without a hitch.

The following day, October 9, was the day of the convocation ceremonies. Traditionally, the academic procession would form up on campus and march down the hill to the Lady Beaverbrook Rink, about one hundred yards outside the university gates. This year, as the faculty section of the procession reached the gates, Norman Strax was waiting. Looking like an avenging angel in his black academic robes, Strax waited in the middle of the road and took his place with the faculty for the procession. As the procession reached the rink, there was a mass of students, many of the radicals holding placards and waving the red flags of revolution and the black flags of anarchy, which just happened also to be the school colours of UNB. The ceremony promised to be an interesting one.

The ceremony is traditionally opened by presidential remarks. I had urged on Mackay the importance of using this as an opportunity to define the nature and purpose of the university as a place that must be isolated from society and where the atmosphere must be conducive to the free exchange of ideas and practice of scholarship. I had hoped that this definition of the purpose of a university could serve to rally the faculty behind these expressed liberal ideals. Mackay accepted my argument and developed what I thought was a very good and very appropriate introductory address.

Unfortunately, no one listened to it as a political statement because the political statement was made instead by Jim Dineen when Colin Mackay rose to begin his remarks. Dineen immediately sprang to his feet in applause, forcing the remainder of the faculty — Norman Strax excepted — to follow suit, as did a number of the students. We were forced to make a commitment to the person of Colin Mackay rather than to his ideals of the university as I had hoped and intended. I felt I had been trapped and very much resented Dineen's action. Mackay's speech passed without notice.

Guest speaker at the convocation was Lord Hartley Shawcross, who had been the chief United Kingdom prosecutor at the Nuremburg trials. Shawcross gave a terrible speech that called for supporting traditional institutional structures whatever the

1968 Fall Convocation. Strax joins the procession, marching behind Theo Weiner.

cost, and was heckled throughout by Nelson Adams, one of the radicals, which offered some comic relief. The ceremony ended without further incident, although the highly charged atmosphere had been exhilarating.

Norman Strax was rarely a direct participant in the further events of that year, yet he became the iconic symbol of the crisis on the campus. Certainly, he was a recognized and vilified figure in the local community and joined Robichaud as a second villain to some sectors of Fredericton society. Strax later claimed he was persecuted by the city police during this period, and he did appear to be continually picked up for various minor motor vehicle infractions. The continuing issue on campus was the question of the proper procedure for Strax's suspension and dismissal. But what Strax had provoked set the stage for other people and organizations to pursue their own agendas. The Strax case became the Strax Affair, which had ramifications at many levels.

Chapter 5
THE ANARCHISM OF LIBERATION 130

For a few weeks in the fall of 1968, the student occupation of "Liberation 130" created an anarchist commune on the UNB campus. Participants in the occupation could imagine they were totally free individuals, outside the reach of any institutional authority and united in defence of their autonomy against external enemies. It was for them a formative experience. For the forty-six days of its existence, until the Remembrance Day weekend in November, public attention, both on the campus and in the media, was focused on Liberation 130 and on the public theatre staged by its occupants.

Over the month and a half of the occupation, the student population of the room varied greatly. Tom Murphy described how it worked. All you had to do was go to the door of Liberation 130 and knock, identify yourself and then go inside and spend some time. Some stayed there most of the time, while others only made token appearances. The occupiers tended to be arts students, many of them honours students, whose appearance in the room was often token because of the pressures of their academic programs.[1] The population of the room increased when there were rumours that the university was about to take direct action to remove the occupants.

Usually about six or seven people stayed for the night. At first, the sit-in was fun. People brought guitars and twenty to twenty-five people would sit around singing. The office was small, so people staying the night had to find floor space to lay out their sleeping bags. Later on, the office was attacked by other students, who threatened violence and threw eggs and rocks at the window, breaking all the glass. The occupants put a piece of plywood over the window, but this cut out most of the light and the room became very dark. The ones who stayed toward the end did so more out of a sense of commitment than a sense of fun.[2]

One of the early occupants of the room was Franz Martin. He arrived in Fredericton on September 8 to enroll as a history major for the year and was assigned to MacKenzie House. I was both the don of his house and the coordinator of the exchange with the University of Maine, so I also acted as his faculty adviser during the year. Martin kept a journal through his year at UNB and this journal allows us insight into some of the thinking and attitudes of the radical camp.

Before coming to UNB, Martin had been working for the American Students for a Democratic Society (SDS) in Maine. He was pleased to find that Lawson Hunter, his proctor, was "quite a radical himself and much more knowledgeable than me." In his second week on campus, Martin discovered a Mobilization literature table in the Student Centre, promptly introduced himself as a worker for the Maine SDS and volunteered to look after the table the following day. By the next night, he was busy making posters for the Mobilization. On September 19, he attended his first Mobilization meeting when "the radical Dr. Strax spoke of his experiences at Columbia and Chicago. Most interesting!" Following the meeting, Martin helped distribute leaflets to inaugurate "bookie-book," "making liberal use of the word Fuck" and advertising a demonstration at the library on the following day. On Friday evening, he went to the library "to help in the ID issues." The library was closed early, and on the way out Martin "defied the ID check. No big thing. But I was there." By Monday, when the third library demonstration took place, Martin had decided that the issue did not interest him. "I can't get excited enough about the ID issue to take an active part and evidently, not many others can either. Strax is going it alone, but I wish him luck!"

When Strax was suspended, however, Martin was indignant. "What kind of a college fires a talented prof. for peaceful dissent?" He went to the Student Centre that evening. "Strax and several of his friends defend themselves. Perhaps converted a few. I'm with them." The next day, Martin cut his first class and joined twenty other people in a demonstration outside the Old Arts Building to protest Strax's dismissal, commenting that "Strax is not very popular campus-wide — because he is such a contro-versial figure."

Martin moved into Liberation 130 when the occupation started on September 27 and slept in the room for the first seven nights. While there, he was visited by four SDS-ers from Maine, who were not impressed. "They were discouraged at the lack of org and anarchistic strain apparent here. No help from them." "What a week," he commented, "No studies at all. I feel free though. It was a very educational experience. Forced to know oneself."[3]

History professor Stephen Patterson visited Liberation 130 in the first week of the occupation. He had been called by one of his students who appeared quite worried and asked him to come to the room so they could talk to him. He went to the room about 6:30 one evening. There were twenty students in the room with Strax, and Patterson felt that the room "already looked like

Inside Liberation 130 in September 1968. Norman Strax is on the telephone. Sitting on the desk to his right is Franz Martin, the exchange student from the University of Maine.

a pigsty," with personal belongings and sleeping bags strewn around the floor. Students were coming and going through the window, and he was told that the bathroom across the hall had already been christened the "Liberation 130 bathroom." Representatives of the media were in the halls outside, covering the story.

Once Patterson got inside the room, he found that the students were concerned about what was likely to happen, but he didn't feel they got much help from him. He was nervous and felt completely out of place. He observed that the students in the room were intelligent, middle class and that many of them came from outside New Brunswick, particularly from anglophone Montreal. He also observed that there appeared to be a disproportionate number of Jewish students. Just as Patterson was about to leave, there was a banging on the door of the room, and when Patterson opened it, he faced the "biggest, burliest weight-lifting kind of guy," leading a group of foresters or geologists who were determined to clean the clocks of the occupants of Liberation 130. As the attacking students pushed on the outside of the door, the students inside pushed the other way and Patterson found himself caught in the door jamb. "At that point," he recalled, "I went into this spiel about the nature of the university and how we don't resolve disputes through the use of violence. This is not how we do things at UNB." Because a CBC reporter had his microphone switched on, Patterson's speech appeared on the national radio news the following day.[4] As he was "rescued" from his predicament by some of the residence faculty, Patterson quipped: "This is what it means to be a man in the middle."

Franz Martin returned to his classes on October 7 after a week spent in Liberation 130. That evening he worked on the demonstration for the Board of Governors' meeting the next day. "A big protest is hoped for but very doubtful since nothing is planned. No co-ordination, no agreement...Disappointing, frustrating." Nevertheless, Martin participated in the sit-in outside the board room. "Scuffle when governors tried to leave. Violent assault by board members and policemen on passive demonstrators."[5]

Although Strax was off campus, campus attention focused on the demonstration in his former office. The occupation was well publicized by the student newspaper, the *Brunswickan*, which covered it extensively and frequently, accompanied by striking photos of the occupants. Editor John Oliver remembered the occasion when George Mossman of the SCM wanted to visit the room and proceeded to climb the ladder to the window, only to be attacked by some engineers who threw food at him when he was half-way up the ladder. The incident was captured on film and appeared in the next issue of the *Brunswickan*.[6] Mackay was not amused that Mossman had been involved with Liberation 130 and phoned Les Shemilt, as chair of the SCM Advisory Board, to let him know. Shemilt, concerned about the future of the SCM on campus, reprimanded Mossman, but regretted it later.[7]

The student body was divided in its reaction to the demonstration. A small number of active demonstrators had the support of a larger number of sympathizers, but there was also a small number of actively hostile opponents. The bulk of the student body at this stage was either indifferent or open-minded. Significantly, the numbers in these groups did not greatly change over the course of the occupation. In fact, the occupation appeared to lose support as people turned their attention to other matters in October and early November.

Some demonstrators, originally without any strong convictions, entered Liberation 130 and found themselves caught up in the intensity of the experience, with its sense of righteousness and its sense of persecution. Tom Murray, an engineering student from Fredericton, was one of these, and he was typical of a number of demonstrators who became involved in the interpersonal dynamics of the Liberation 130 experience.[8]

Within the core group, some activists were attracted by the action and the excitement of the occasion. Richard Archer had been unsuccessful in his first year at UNB, and in 1968 had enrolled as a student at the provincial Teachers' College. He had been a resident of MacKenzie House when he was at UNB, and my impression of him then was that he had little sense of direction or purpose. He appeared in Liberation 130 and was not, I believe, very popular in that group, where he was continually urging the group to take action of one kind or another. Another example was Dan Weston, from Oromocto, whom I did not know well, except that he was reputedly one of the more active radicals. My impression of Weston at the time was that of a burly man who liked to parade about the campus in knee-high boots, looking suitably revolutionary.

Archer and Weston struck me — perhaps unfairly — as the kind of revolutionaries who were more interested in the action itself and who might just as well have fit into a right-wing demonstration as a left-wing one. Having interviewed Weston for this book and getting to know him better at the time, I was struck by his Marxist analysis of the crisis around the Strax Affair, the only such analysis I heard from any of the former student radicals that I interviewed. Weston has also remained true to his values through his career in Fredericton as the driving force behind FAPO, the Fredericton Anti-Poverty Organization.[9]

Franz Martin was frequently dismayed and frustrated by the inability of the group — the SDS or the Mobilization SDS as he refers to it — to make and carry out decisions. He often felt that the men of action in the group diverted attention by wanting to act without much thought or planning. After Strax was forced to leave the campus, Martin became one of his contacts and confidants inside the room. On the day after the fall convocation, Strax told him that he wanted the SDS reorganized. "Good God!," Martin commented in his journal, "so do I but with nothing to start on — Chaos." When Martin took some things to Strax at the campus gate the next day he found him "eternally optimistic." Yet, Martin was pessimistic and continued to be dismayed by the lack of organization in the SDS. On October 20, he went to a meeting at Strax's camp, "way out in the woods," where "several decisions made and the radical org. [sic] grows stronger." A meeting on the following Friday night after distributing leaflets around town was "chaos…Everyone tired and wanting or needing a break from tension over the weekend." They talked about picketing the US Consulate in Saint John on the following day. "Killed, I guess. No decisions. Broke up in disgust." In Liberation 130 later that night, there was much talk about taking action on campus, such as occupying the Old Arts Building.

The next day Franz missed an SDS meeting but learned that the group had decided to occupy Allen Boone's office and other rooms in Bailey Hall until Strax's injunction was lifted. "Packed my 'sit-in kit'…toothbrush, aspirin, apple, camera and film, paper and homework. Set out prepared to act only to be told that the plan was off." Later that day, there was talk of occupying the president's office, but only seven people were willing to take the risk. "Many fear instant expulsion. Great pressure. Indecision. Hesitancy. Gradually others drop out. I am convinced we are not prepared, mentally or materially. Some few will go, but only as a sort of obligation to 'cause.' No idea of what they are doing or hope to gain. The weaknesses of SDS glare now."[10]

Practising existential politics, the occupants of Liberation 130 were not to be diverted from their actions by either faculty or administrative representatives or even by their non-demonstrating student sympathizers. These sympathizers tended to fall into two categories. In one group were the civil libertarians, including a large number of honours and graduate students, particularly in the arts faculty. These students did not want to demonstrate themselves, but they were prepared to protect the right of the students occupying Liberation 130 to do so. On hearing a rumour that the president was about to press legal charges against the students in the room or to expel them from the university, a petition was drawn up and signed by a good number of honours and graduate students saying that they would accept for themselves any punishment that was given out to the students in Liberation 130.

The other group of non-participating sympathizers was the student politicians, most notably Lawson Hunter, who visited the room a number of times and sought to advise the demonstrators and to channel their energies towards political gains.[11] Yet while the occupation continued, these student politicians were continually frustrated, as power continued to rest with the occupiers who refused to be directed from outside. They believed and practised "participatory democracy," and in their anarchic fashion would not be tied to anyone else's organizational schemes. This is the reason the demonstrators could never organize sufficiently to acquire greater public support while the occupation was in progress.

Hunter and I frequently met in the evening in my apartment in MacKenzie House and discussed the events on campus. I would inform him how I saw events developing and he, in turn, would tell me how he interpreted them. This gave me a good feel for the political views of various factions, and I felt it important that Hunter should also be informed of the views of those parties with whom I was in touch. Mackay did not trust Hunter and was rather wary of my own connection with him. The threat that Mackay hinted at but never carried through was that Hunter was not trustworthy as a proctor, but Hunter proved entirely professional in his approach to the proctorship, and I had no complaints with him on that score.

I also kept channels open with other radical students I knew. The result was that I would occasionally get late-evening visits from various radicals, who would come to talk or to find out what was going on. The division and lack of trust between left-wing students was brought home to me graphically one evening in my residence apartment. Lawson Hunter was visiting when a knock came on the door, and Dan Lingemann appeared. Lingemann was a graduate student in history and a rather fuzzy socialist-cum-civil-libertarian. Lingemann and Hunter had little to say to one another, so I found myself carrying the conversation. Another knock and Tom Murphy arrived from Liberation 130, for some apparent purpose. When he saw Hunter and Lingemann, however, he would not say anything either. The result was that the four of us talked around the issues and I could not draw any of them out. When they left, I was none the wiser about why they had come.

During the occupation, it was the practice on Friday or Saturday nights for a particularly successful drinking event to be crowned by an attempt by a drunken mob to tear the radicals out of Liberation 130. Geology, business administration and forestry students attempted this at various times. While many of these students were just along for the fun of it, there usually tended to be one or two "red-necked" leaders who were intent on beating up or otherwise injuring the demonstrators whom they claimed were a disgrace to the university. One geologist almost got in the window of 130 with a rock axe before his ladder was pushed away from the building. Another tried to get in with a lead pipe.

One of the reasons these demonstrations did not culminate in more serious violence and injury was because of the action of the men's residence faculty and students. As the men's residences overlooked Bailey Hall, we were frequently called in when there was an attack on Liberation 130, and we would use our influence to stop the attackers and convince them that their energies could be better directed elsewhere. Usually a trouble-spot on campus, the men's residences were unusually quiet and content in 1968–69. One of the reasons for this was the excellent job that sociologist Brent McKeown had done as acting dean of men's residence since 1967. Personally open and friendly, he had given students the impression that the residence administration and faculty were on their side and had welded the faculty dons and resident fellows together into a comfortable team who enjoyed each other's company. McKeown also had the ability to deal with Colin Mackay, who respected his effectiveness and gave him his head in managing the residences.

Along with myself, McKeown was one of the younger faculty members who were well known by the student radicals. Consequently, he had followed the affair closely and was sympathetic to many of the demonstrating students. When violence threatened at Bailey Hall, McKeown would rally the residence faculty and those of us who were about would wade into the fray. I remember going out myself, along with Gord Myers, the financial aid officer who was the don of Bridges House; Doug Ruthven, chemical engineer and don of Jones House; Phil Buckner, the historian who was don of Neville; and Peter MacRae, an

Anglican priest-cum-sociologist, who was don of Aitken House. Occasionally, student proctors would also help out.

The residence faculty and students, in fact, did the work around Liberation 130 that was not being done by either the UNB Security Police or the student Campus Police. One security officer was permanently stationed in Bailey Hall, but his job was only to keep an eye on university property, so he had very little to do with Liberation 130 other than to observe. Security policemen were conspicuous by their absence when there was any threat of mob violence.

Franz Martin had a key to Liberation 130 and quite often was the lone occupant of the room when the others were at an SDS meeting off campus. Toward the end of October, the attacks on Liberation 130 became more frequent. On October 28 he noted: "About 100 drunks. Invasion by ladder @ window, after a barrage of rocks and beer bottles, and by door using cement ashtray as battering ram." While the window assault was repelled when the students inside got the ladder, the attackers "injected a mild tear gas under the door which stung eyes but not seriously." Martin arrived at the room at 11:00 pm, by which time the mob was gone. "Dispersed by P.C. Kent and other liberals." The room occupants then repaired the broken door by replacing it with the door from the next office, as more occupants arrived for the night. "Lib 130 perseveres," noted Martin. "Those people have guts!"

The SDS struck back the following night with "provo guerrilla tactics," spray-painting slogans around the campus. Then there was another attack on Liberation 130 by about fifty people on October 30. "It had been quite a fight. All windows broken out this time! Another ladder had been used and was also seized by the defenders. Now we have 2!!" "Too bad — one of the attackers was sent to hospital when struck in face with stick by a defender. I hate to see anyone hurt but — would he have hesitated to hurt us? I think not...and so it escalates — Hate grows. What a world."

Brent McKeown and Steve Patterson dissuade students outside Liberation 130.

A big attack was expected on Halloween. According to Martin, Liberation 130 was "clear and clean and prepared for battle." The attack began at 8:00 pm. "Those who can't stay are out — the door locked, barred, chained. Oh yes the floor outside has been smeared with grease...A whoop and they charge down the hill. Rocks and eggs thud against protective screen. All glass long since broken. Lights out, water running to freshen air — we wait in muted attitudes. 200 attackers at peak. A guy outside with walkie-talkie keeps us informed. They drift away after storming up ladders as before...A few come back periodically to throw garbage. A canister of foul acid bursts and permeates room with stench. Some of us leave, nauseated. The worst is over." Later that night, a water pipe burst at about 4:00 am, flooding the office and dripping into the faculty office below.[12]

The significance of the absence of Security Police or the Campus Police was brought home to me that night. Brent McKeown had left earlier in the day to go to Montreal to attend a conference at Loyola College on student use and abuse of drugs. I was due to attend the same conference and to fly out later in the evening. Gordon Myers, the don of Bridges House, was

A guard in the window of Liberation 130, October 1968.

being left in charge of the residences on what was traditionally one of the wildest nights of the year.

As I was packing after supper, Gord called me to say that Liberation 130 was being attacked. I left my packing and helped him fend off some marauders. I then saw a student member of the Campus Police passing. I asked him where his colleagues were and why they weren't on duty at Bailey Hall. He said the Campus Police was assigned to protect Lady Dunn Hall, the women's residence, from Halloween pranksters. I went to Lady Dunn and met one of the Campus Police who lived in MacKenzie House. He told me that they had clear orders from Chief Barnett to stay away from Bailey Hall that night.

I was furious. When I returned to Fredericton from the drug conference, I sent a memo to Vice-President Macaulay complaining about the reluctance of Barnett to provide adequate protection at Bailey Hall. I suggested that there appeared to be a concerted plan to let the hooligans terminate the demonstration, which was only being foiled by the activity of the residence faculty. My memo was never answered.

The official administrative response to the occupation was a patient one, presumably letting events take what course they would. There was a reasonable amount of sympathy for the demonstrating students among some administrators, especially Registrar Dugald Blue, Dean of Science Bill Argue and myself, who advised the president to let the demonstration run its course and let the students vacate the room of their own volition. One morning Mackay sent the three of us to speak to the demonstrators. We were received at the door of 130 and told to wait while the students decided whether or not they wished to receive us. They finally informed us that they would only receive me. Blue and Argue had to cool their heels in the hallway outside while I entered the room and made a case for their ending the occupation and they, in turn, explained politely why they could not. It was a futile visit.

The tactics of patience did not pay off, however, and the continuation of the demonstration meant that the university would eventually have to take other steps to end the occupation. Looking back on these events with the benefit of hindsight and assessing the role of power and propaganda in the occupation of Room 130, I can see that the appropriate and expected response to that kind of demonstration was the exercise of countervailing force and propaganda by the university. I was not prepared to accept that in 1968, partly because I didn't really understand the nature of the commitment the demonstrating students had made. Those students were prepared to stand by their commitment and were prepared to accept whatever violence and injury was meted out to them as part of that commitment. Naively I had hoped to protect them from such consequences, when they themselves had decided they could not avoid them. I was also not prepared to accept the logical counter-reaction, because this polarization of the university community was abhorrent to my idea of what a university was supposed to be about.

I had defined my own position as being very much in the centre of the political spectrum, and I had worked during the previous three years to bring students and faculty together in comfortable discourse. I had tried to do this in residence and in my teaching. I had hoped to use my influence as Mackay's assistant to further this cause. I had welcomed the teach-ins of the previous year along with the heightened political consciousness of the students as a great opportunity for developing a more-aware and sensitive student body. I had hoped that this could raise the general level of campus discourse and help to make classes and seminars real centres of intellectual stimulation.

I was mistaken. One of the greatest disappointments of that year was to observe how the students moved out of their deferential, good-natured apathy to greater awareness of society and politics, and just as quickly, into rigid unthinking ideological stances, where dogma replaced discussion. Discussion, in fact, was ridiculed by the radicals as one of the stalling tactics of the unthinking and unfeeling liberals.

The one place where I insisted that channels for discussion be kept open was in MacKenzie House. I felt that it was important that students who lived in MacKenzie House not be subjected to pressure to commit themselves to one camp or another so that they could look on the place as a sanctuary from external politics. Politics would be discussed but in an open fashion. This was particularly important because of my role as the president's assistant and because Lawson Hunter was very involved in planning radical strategies. My other proctor, Alfred Brien, was also a law student but preferred to remain on the political sidelines. Many members of the house were highly politicized, but I was satisfied that all views were represented and that the residents felt free to discuss the issues with one another.

It was the political centre that appeared to be weakest during the year. While members of the faculty had a knowledge and understanding of the student position and working together had influenced decisions by the board and president, nevertheless one of the reasons for the apparent weakness of the centre were the rifts that existed within the faculty. The faculty members on the board had hoped to preserve reasoned discussion of the Strax case with the AUNBT and with the faculty generally, but history professor Murray Young found that events got beyond them and that the result was faculty polarization. In particular, Young claimed that it had been irresponsible for Mackay to take out the injunction when he did.[13]

The faculty effectively divided into right and left wings. The right wing consisted of those who felt that the proper stance at this time was unswerving loyalty to the president. It was immoral to use Mackay's discomfiture to seek advantage in traditional quarrels that the faculty had had with him. Perhaps the most vocal Mackay loyalist was the dean of engineering, Jim Dineen. Dineen expressed his views and position clearly and strongly at AUNBT meetings and he led many members of the engineering faculty in their active support of the president. Alfred Bailey, the vice-president (academic), a radical of the 1930s and one of the great builders and innovators in the modern university, was horrified by the Strax demonstration. Bailey, as honorary librarian, had steadily worked to build up the library as the centre of research and scholarship on the campus. He was very upset that Strax and his fellow protestors showed so little respect for learning that they were prepared to force the closure of the main repository of the learning of the ages, and thus to stop the university from performing its proper function. To Bailey, this action was akin to the Nazi book-burnings of the 1930s and must never be tolerated in a liberal society. Strax deserved no sympathy.

Associate Professor of Physics Theo Weiner also disliked Strax's radicalism and what it portended. Weiner had already experienced where radicalism could take a society in Nazi Germany, and since his wife Roberta was in charge of the circulation desk at the library, he had seen her being forced to deal with the Strax protest. Generally, the right-wing of the faculty consisted of those, normally in the applied sciences, who were concerned about the public image of the university and who felt that this was a time for strong demonstrations of corporate loyalty. The other element of this right-wing consisted of those from various faculties who disapproved so strongly of what Strax had done that they could see no reason to show him any sympathy or to be concerned about his rights.

Economics professor John Earl claimed that there was almost an atmosphere of lynching on campus. Sitting in the Faculty Club after the demonstrations began, Earl tells the story of overhearing a group of senior faculty, mostly from the applied side, "talking about it and the word 'Jew' was thrown around and the word 'foreigner.' If this guy didn't like it here, why the hell didn't he get out and go back where he came from? It was obvious that these people weren't sympathetic to any sort of reasonable approach to it," claimed Earl.[14]

The faculty left-wing consisted of liberals rather than radicals. Strax himself received very little personal support or sympathy from members of the faculty, most of whom disapproved of the nature and location of his demonstration. Those who did give him direct support, like business administration professor Harold Sharp, saw the discomfiture of Mackay and the polarization of the institution as a situation from which the faculty could derive more power, better terms of employment and a more effective role for their association, the AUNBT.

Many of the left-wing did not want the university to be polarized and directed their energies to preventing the president and the radical students from tearing the institution apart. Some tried to end the occupation and to transfer the protest to political channels, where much needed reforms could be brought about. A large group of faculty met secretly one night in the Sheldrick Room, the history seminar room in Carleton Hall, to discuss tactics. About a hundred people crowded into a relatively small room, many sitting on the floor. Earl, Sharp and Patterson were there, as were a number of people from the English department. Some members of the AUNBT executive also participated. As Patterson recalled, there was more than one agenda in the room. "Some people were concerned about the students. Some were concerned about the moral issue of Strax and his rights and some were interested in making use of the events of the time to propel the university into the modern era, unionize and create a broader participation of the faculty in the institution." When they discussed Mackay, "the feeling was general that whatever individuals thought about Colin, it was common agreement that he had to go. He wasn't handling this situation correctly, but more than that, there were other problems that had to do with the management of the institution and the proper role the faculty should play in the institution."[15]

A number of us worked to heal the polarization. I attended one meeting with Les Shemilt, Kent Thompson, Brent McKeown and a couple of others to consider what might be done. Murray Young saw his role on the Board of Governors as trying to hold the centre together. We received little sympathy for our efforts. Many of the left-wing were in the arts and science faculties and our intentions were misinterpreted by the right-wing faculty as disloyalty to the president and the institution. From both poles, we were discredited as "wishy-washy liberals."

The damage that this faculty polarization did to the institution was enormous. It was unpleasant in 1968–69 to attend faculty parties because you immediately looked around, once you were inside the door, to see who were your friends and who were your enemies. Old friendships among faculty members were destroyed over the issue. As late as 1980, the faculty remained scarred by the mistrust associated with the events of eleven years before. The engineers still looked for revolutionaries in the arts faculty, and members of the arts faculty still regarded many engineers as political dinosaurs.

The continued existence of Liberation 130 was a manifestation of the continuing conflict on campus and the president finally decided to bring it to an end in early November. The room would be emptied swiftly and professionally on the weekend of Remembrance Day, when most of the students had gone home for the long weekend. At 4:00 am on Saturday, November 10, the Fredericton City Police arrived on campus, removed the door of Liberation 130, and dragged the remaining protestors out of the room. Once the room had been cleared, the door and window were boarded up and a security man was placed on guard. The occupants of the room were taken off campus to the police station, and subsequently released by the police. Few people were aware of what was happening.

The ending of the occupation ended the anarchist phase of the affair. The student and faculty politicians now took up where the radicals had been forced to leave off, and far greater organization, direction and purpose was given to the subsequent development of the affair.

Chapter 6
INCREASING TENSIONS

The closing of Liberation 130 took the leadership of the student protest away from Mobilization SDS and the occupants of Strax's former office and created a new opportunity for the politicians of the Student's Representative Council. The activist climate on campus resulted in the election of a much more radical SRC in early November, which immediately took up the mandate of confronting the president and the university administration. Yet, while the council was activist, it lacked consistent leadership, which undermined its effectiveness in representing the student voice.

David Cox was one of the casualties of the "Liberation 130" period as SRC President. In October, Cox was finding his presidential role progressively more difficult. He was not in sympathy with the radicals but was facing pressure from a number of directions to take the leadership of the student protest. At SRC meetings, Cox felt he was constantly being criticized by radicals like David Hallam, Bronwyn McIntyre, John Oliver and Lawson Hunter, and was also being attacked in the *Brunswickan* as "incompetent, incapable and insensitive." He was losing control of the SRC meetings where, he felt, anarchy usually reigned. Realizing that his academic work was likely to suffer and finding his presidency progressively less congenial, Cox resigned at the end of October. He did so reluctantly, feeling that his resignation had let his supporters down, and when he was interviewed in 2000, Cox, then a senior executive with Bell Canada, concluded that this particular resignation was the hardest decision he had ever made in his life, "and if I had to do it again, I wouldn't do it."[1]

New SRC elections were held on November 6, and Geoffrey Green, a fourth-year psychology student, was elected president with a council that was far more radical than its conservative predecessor. It was the radical nature of this new council that set the direction of student politics for the next two or three months. Green himself was an enigma. He appeared out of the blue when he was nominated for the presidency, having shown no previous interest in student politics. He had not been associated with the radicals, nor was he known to be an academic heavyweight. He was enrolled in the Regular Officer's Training Plan (ROTP) and was, therefore, going through the university on a military scholarship. I found him difficult to approach, partly because he didn't seem to have much conception of the job of SRC president but also because, with the election of the new council, the SRC veered onto a radical course and Green seemed to enjoy his new-found role as radical leader.

It was on the weekend after Green's election that Liberation 130 was "busted." In his journal, Franz Martin recorded that the end of Liberation 130 meant he had an opportunity to catch up on his study and essay-writing, and it also forced the SDS to reorganize its Fredericton operation. "SDS is in trouble," he noted. "Cop outs, including myself to some degree. Lack of vigour. The group morale is high, though all are tired and tense." While the SDS could only attract the "old stand bys" to their meetings, which Martin found "depressing," he was impressed by the way that the SRC had now sprung to life. "They are amazingly militant since the recent elections. It does my heart good."[2]

The new council went on the offensive at its meeting of November 17 by calling for the president and the Board of Deans to attend a public meeting with the SRC in three days' time to explain why the City Police had been called on campus to terminate Liberation 130.[3] This demand for a public meeting was a tactical move, with the support and encouragement of Lawson Hunter.[4] Given the immediacy of the meeting and the peremptory nature of the SRC demand, the Board of Deans found the request unacceptable, but they did leave the door open for a meeting at a mutually agreed time.[5]

Franz Martin was ecstatic about the planned public meeting "to face questions re Strax, cops on campus, security cops, etc. The whole bag. Isn't it great!" Everyone, he felt, was now talking about student power. "Mostly re SRC, not SDS but considering the total apathy 3 months ago and the only 'general' apathy now, I'd say we are gaining some small victories." The SRC was taking the lead in challenging Mackay and the deans, so Martin mused: "SDS must go along quietly for a while. SRC has money and influence; we don't. Support them to a point. But I still don't trust them."[6]

The meeting was advertised by the SRC and opened as scheduled on Wednesday, November 20, in the main auditorium of the arts building with Lawson Hunter in the chair. The auditorium was packed with students, but there was no sign of the deans. The SRC then voted to make another request for a special meeting with the Board of Deans under the threat that "if the Board of Deans do not appear at a meeting by midnight on the 28th of November, 1968; the SRC will call for and organize a general strike of the University community."[7]

A number of students were very upset by the absence of the

deans from this meeting. Some of them had been unsympathetic to Strax and the radicals but now were becoming politicized. "Why won't the deans speak to our student representatives?" asked one engineering student from MacKenzie House. "What have they got to hide?" He dismissed my argument that the SRC was playing confrontation politics and that the deans could not be expected to appear. He held nothing against the deans, he said, but he did want to hear their side of the story. If they would not appear, then it could only confirm the rumours that they were not concerned with the welfare of the students.

***

The National Council of the CAUT met in Montreal on the weekend of November 16–17, when James B. Milner, the chair of the Academic Freedom and Tenure Committee, introduced discussion on the "Case of Professor Norman Strax." He reported that Strax had still not received any statement of the charges against him, nor had he been offered the opportunity of a hearing as requested by the CAUT executive. Doug Brewer responded that this statement was a bit premature, since the AUNBT had not yet even addressed the matter and were waiting until the facts had been made known by the McAllister Committee.

George McAllister sprang to the defence of the university and claimed that "the reasons for the suspension had in fact been stated, though not at the time when the action was taken." The court action taken against Strax was not on the suspension but rather on the charge of trespass, where the university had acted in a responsible manner. McAllister especially objected to the fact that the CAUT executive was getting its information "from representatives of Professor Strax, but not from the internal investigating committee, whose report was now available." McAllister did not convince the CAUT Council, which ended its meeting by condemning the action of UNB "in suspending a faculty member without stated charges or provisions for an adjudicative hearing."[8]

The AUNBT had not met since the Strax Affair had begun. Some members had little faith that Mackay or the Board of Governors would treat Strax fairly and felt that CAUT involvement was the only way to make them respect Strax's rights. Ed Maher, the head of the program in business administration, had bitterly opposed Mackay for years, looking on him "as the source of all evil at UNB." Maher was well connected with the CAUT and the New Democratic Party, but in 1968–69 he was on sabbatical leave in central Canada and was not an obvious protagonist in the events of that year.[9]

The initiative from inside the UNB faculty to involve the CAUT was taken by close colleagues of Maher: business professor Harold Sharp; economist John Earl; and Perry Robinson, the head of philosophy, who had gone directly to the CAUT executive.[10] "I supplied you and the committee with all the material I had on the Strax case when I was in Montreal," Harold Sharp wrote to Percy Smith, executive secretary of the CAUT. "In addition, I expressed my opinion on the matter to you, and part of the Milner committee. At that time, I emphasized it was my opinion and that it might be biased. However, I felt, and still feel, that I was as honest and objective as anyone could be under the circumstances."[11]

Later, Sharp shared with Smith his perspective on the faculty members of the Board of Governors. Of the board members, he deemed Murray Young to be "probably the most trustworthy," commenting that he was "generally considered to be a reasonable and honest individual who is inclined to be a liberal." The other faculty members did not fare so well in his assessment. He felt that George McAllister would do anything "to curry favour with those who have the authority to appoint him dean of law," if and when Bill Ryan, the current dean, is appointed to the bench. Les Shemilt was "generally considered to be a smooth operator and very ambitious," and Eric Garland was also "engaged in climbing the UNB ladder," and "like Shemilt he is inclined to say what you want to hear."[12]

Like George McAllister, Desmond Pacey, the dean of graduate studies, did not think the CAUT was getting the UNB story straight. Pacey wrote a personal letter to his old friend C. Brough Macpherson, the Marxist political theorist and professor of political economy at the University of Toronto who was also the current president of the CAUT. "Dr. Strax was suspended for reasons which were perfectly obvious to him and to everyone else who knew what went on in our library in late September," wrote Pacey, who denied most strongly that Strax had been suspended because of his opposition to the Vietnam War. Strax had had his contract continued for a further year in spite of dissatisfaction with his teaching "because we knew that if he was let go everyone would assume that his political unorthodoxy was the real cause."[13]

The members of the UNB faculty were in a serious dilemma that fall. They disapproved of what Strax had done in the library and with the way he had encouraged students to disrupt the studies of others. They felt that Strax was using a non-issue, that of the ID cards, to stir up trouble on campus. Many faculty members also felt sympathy for Mackay, who was trying to deal with the difficult situation created by Strax while keeping the university functioning in a normal fashion. There was little faculty sympathy for Strax yet, because the matter had been discussed by the CAUT, and the issue of respect for faculty rights had been raised. Most faculty members initially felt that the reason for Strax's suspension was so obvious that it did not have to be spelled out, but, slowly and somewhat reluctantly, many came to believe that he did deserve some sort of adjudicative review of his case, if only to

Harold Sharp, Associate Professor of Business.

establish the principle of the proper way of terminating a faculty appointment.

These faculty divisions surfaced on November 26, at the first general meeting of the AUNBT to discuss the Strax Affair. In an attempt to bridge divisions in its membership, the association's executive had prepared a motion reflecting the various positions that people subscribed to in the hope of shaping some kind of consensus. The result, however, was a clunky motion, whose goals and meaning were unclear. The motion first deplored the delay of the administration in establishing "prompt and just pro-cedures" for investigating and adjudicating the charges against Strax. It condemned the "precipitous and continuing resort" to legal proceedings as an "abdication by the university of its proper authority." At the same time, it also deplored "any deliberate obstruction by individuals of the proper business of the univer-sity" in an attempt to circumvent established university channels. The motion called on the university administration to return "any outstanding cases of possible student or faculty misconduct" to within the University's "various governing bodies" and to institute proper adjudication in these cases. Finally, it threatened that, if this action is not carried out, the AUNBT should "vote non-confidence" in those branches of the administration that have failed to act in this way.[14]

According to Doug Brewer, this motion was "an attempt to steer a middle course," but he later commented that "it was interesting to see both 'left' and 'right' wings unite in opposition against it." The motion was approved by a split vote of sixty-one in favour and forty-two opposed. Many members felt that the motion was too strong and proposed amendments to soften it, but these were all defeated.[15]

Mackay was furious when he received the AUNBT motion, which indicated to him that the association was lining up in support of the CAUT. He presented Brewer with a list of objections and questions arising from the motion. Any delay, claimed Mackay, was not the fault of the board, but rather of the AUNBT, which had asked for more time to study the report of the McAllister Committee. In his rant, Mackay felt that the board would interpret the AUNBT motion as meaning that they should never resort to court action in dealing with a faculty member. Because of his anger at the AUNBT motion, Mackay was prepared to ignore the AUNBT as a player as the Strax Affair developed; the AUNBT was not invited to participate in any subsequent discussions of the Board of Governors.

Faced with these strong objections, Brewer decided to take the motion back to the executive for further clarification; "otherwise I feel the AUNBT might be made to look rather silly, since the motion, in the legal sense, is meaningless."[16] The AUNBT executive however, wanted to send the motion directly to the Board of Governors while not releasing it to the public;[17] other members of the AUNBT leaked the original draft to the *Brunswickan* and to the local CBC radio station.[18]

The hearings on the Strax injunction took place, as scheduled, in Barry's courtroom in Saint John in November. Don Gilliss and Bill Hoyt appeared for the university, and Duff Harper and Vincent Kelly of the Ontario Bar appeared for Strax. Strax's lawyers denied the allegations of the University and the legality of Strax's suspension. They also claimed that the UNB Board of Governors had never authorized Mackay to obtain the injunction.

Tom Murphy was a regular contributor to the *Brunswickan*, with a column called "Jelly Beans" in 1967–68 and "Spades Down" in 1968.[19] Because of his involvement in Liberation 130, Murphy was asked to testify for the defence in the Strax trial in late November. Vincent Kelly asked him to come to Saint John, along with other witnesses, including Chief Librarian Gertrude Gunn. When Justice Barry found that Kelly had asked Gunn to testify but had not advised the prosecution in advance, he evicted Kelly from the case.

Murphy was incensed. "The system was stacked against this professor. He had a witness and then he lost his lawyer, and then what more can be done?"[20] Murphy went directly home and wrote his column for the December 3 *Brunswickan*. In the column, he recounted his experience in Barry's courtroom, which he claimed was "a mockery of justice," being biased against Strax. Murphy then castigated Barry for the manner in which he had dismissed Vincent Kelly, and concluded:

The courts in New Brunswick are simply the instruments of the corporate elite. Their duty is not so much to make just decisions as to make right decisions (i.e. decisions which will further perpetuate the elite which controls and rewards them.) Court appointments are political appointments. Only the naïve would reject the notion that an individual becomes a justice or judge after he proves his worth to the establishment.[21]

As Murphy commented later, "My motivation was to report what was, for me, an outrage. You can't believe how offended I was about what was going on; it struck me as being utterly unfair. This guy wasn't being given a chance."

On November 26, the Board of Deans gave the SRC written reasons for removing the students from "Liberation 130," which included "the strain and annoyance caused to those who work in the building, the fact that this 'sit-in' had become a focus for unrest, that damage had been caused, although not necessarily by the occupants, and the known presence of people who were not students, particularly in a building which is normally locked at night." Since the action had been taken to end the situation and not to punish, the board had not pressed charges against the students who had been in the room. The deans offered to meet the SRC if such a meeting was "still considered desirable and necessary."[22]

While the deans made no mention of the threat of a general student strike, this threat had not been lost on the provincial media. The *King's County Record* of November 28 responded that "to make the failure of university officials to thumb their noses at the law an excuse for a strike is nothing but an attempt to enforce anarchy upon the university. There can be only one course of action open to the university if a strike takes place — close the university for the balance of the college year. If you want an education, we'll provide it. If you don't please tell us, so we can stop wasting your time, our time, and the public's money."[23]

Before the meeting with the deans could take place, Geoff Green suddenly resigned as SRC president, stating no particular reason for doing so. Rumour had it that the army had not been pleased with his election and had forced his resignation with the threat of otherwise losing his ROTP scholarship. Green was succeeded by his vice-president, Alastair Robertson, who became acting president on December 1 and remained in that job until his own resignation in February 1969. Robertson, a Scot with degrees from St. Andrews University, was a resident of MacKenzie House who had entered UNB in 1967 to pursue a doctorate in English. He had taught school for some years and was close to thirty in 1968. Robertson's most notable feature was his loquaciousness. It was a standard joke around MacKenzie House that, if you got caught in conversation by Alastair, it would be at least three hours before you could disengage yourself. Alastair's conversations were also very one-sided — he talked and you listened. In the fall of 1968, Alastair became progressively more radical. He had sought to control and direct the radicals of Liberation 130 during the fall convocation demonstrations, only to be rebuffed by them. Now, as acting president of the SRC, he was in a position to direct the student protest, and this seemed to substantiate his conception of himself as Danton or Robespierre or Trotsky. He played the part to the hilt.

One of Robertson's assets as SRC president was his age and academic seniority as a doctoral student, which gave him credibility with faculty and senior administrators. He was close to Desmond Pacey, the head of English and dean of graduate studies. Even though the deadline for the meeting with the deans had passed, the SRC under Robertson rescinded its motion calling for a general strike and agreed to meet the deans at its next

Mackay is confronted in the student cafeteria, February 1969.

regular meeting on Sunday, December 8.[24] With reassurances from Robertson, the president and the deans agreed to attend the meeting.

Mobilization SDS continued to meet through November, preparing demands and action plans in the event of a student strike. After Geoff Green resigned, Franz Martin noted: "What a screwed up mess, what a fiasco to learn that SRC has completely copped out. Has given Board of Deans one more week to answer charges. By word of A. Robertson, acting pres, I assume. The bastard! Certainly no strike now."[25]

The meeting between the Board of Deans and the SRC on December 8 was one of the most tense and unpleasant events of that year. It was an exercise in student power, where the president and the deans had been called to account before a radical student council. It was convened in the large business case room of Tilley Hall. The president and the Board of Deans sat around a table in the centre of the room, with President Mackay at one end. Facing them were the members of the SRC. Lawson Hunter chaired the meeting and the questions were asked by Acting

President Robertson, relishing his role as "Grand Inquisitor." The rest of the room was packed with a student audience, sensing the importance of this exercise in student power.

The SRC wanted to know the circumstances surrounding the removal of the students from Liberation 130 by the Fredericton police. Why was it decided to end the sit-in in early November? Had the students in the room been warned and what alternative actions had been considered? The questions were answered primarily by Mackay, who explained that the university had used the Fredericton City Police in order to remove the students from the room in the most effective and efficient manner possible, recognizing that neither the Security Police nor the Campus Police had been trained for this type of activity. The university solicitors had made the arrangements and only they knew when the police would act. Because there were a number of non-students occupying Liberation 130, this was no longer a matter that could be dealt with through the normal internal processes of the university. People had been removed from the room without violence. While charges had initially been laid against the students and non-students, these were being dropped because the main goal of the university had been to clear the room of its occupiers.

The discussion was civil and focused, but the tension in the crowded room was palpable. It was made more so when, in the middle of the meeting, the dean of law, William Ryan, in what appeared to be a reaction to the tension, threw up on the table and had to leave the meeting. The significance of this meeting, apart from an effort by Mackay to answer the student questions pretty directly, lay in the event itself, in the president and deans of the university being called to explain themselves to the student council. It was good political theatre, but it didn't really lead anywhere and only served to embitter relations between the president and the SRC. After this event, Mackay became suspicious of all student motives as they sought to play some role in the operation of the university.

In December, Harold Sharp sent Doug Brewer's AUNBT summary of the November CAUT meeting to CAUT Executive Secretary Percy Smith, claiming that it was an inaccurate summary that distorted the substance of the meeting. Sharp objected to the fact that Brewer had questioned whether the CAUT had been accurately informed of the situation at UNB. Sharp also objected to the fact that George McAllister had indicated that the CAUT was receiving information from the "representatives of Prof. Strax." Sharp asked Smith to send Brewer "a suitable summary of the Montreal meetings and a copy of the motions passed by the National Council with a request that he circulate the material to our faculty."

A week later, acting as Sharp had requested and in some embarrassment at having to reprimand one of the university faculty associations, Smith wrote to Brewer, telling him that he was disturbed by the statement in Brewer's summary suggesting that the CAUT had been accepting facts "from representatives of Professor Strax" but not from the internal UNB investigating committee. Smith wondered whether Brewer "should not consider making a statement to your members that would clarify the sentence in your report to which I have referred."[26] Brewer appears to have ignored this request.

***

This gathering tension in November and December reached a climax at the board meeting of December 19, when Colin Mackay stunned the meeting by announcing his intention to resign the presidency effective June 30, 1969. The meeting immediately struck a small committee of board members, led by K.C. Irving, to consult with Mackay. They recommended at the end of the meeting that the board should accept the resignation and begin the process for his replacement by naming an acting president designate. When Mackay's resignation had been accepted by Premier Robichaud, the board should then appoint a committee to select a new president, in accordance with the terms of the *UNB Act.*

The resignation shocked the university because in many ways it was unlike Mackay; he was a fighter, not a quitter. There is no question that he had been under enormous pressure since the Strax Affair started, and given the nature of his autocratic style, he had become the target and the symbol of oppression to the campus radicals. He was "the administration."

After the news of the resignation emerged, I asked Mackay why he had resigned. He explained that the University had changed with the 1968 *University Act.* It had become a much more consultative institution with various interests to be given a hearing all the time and he did not feel that that was the university he was used to working with. Times change, he said, and it was time for him to move along. "I'm not a good democrat," he told me, as he explained that the new university government required a president who would function well as a committee man. He had just turned fifty, and there was still time for him to develop another career. He had been planning to resign anyway, and the events of the past term had only decided the timing of his decision.

On the other hand, some people felt that Mackay originally had no intention of leaving but, by his offer to resign, was seeking a vote of confidence in his leadership from the board. One member of the board felt that it would have willingly given him that vote as a demonstration of loyalty, so distressed were they at the prospect of the president resigning in the middle of the Strax crisis. This board member credited K.C. Irving with the wisdom to see that it was time for a change. It was Irving's sub-committee

Colin Mackay signing diplomas.

which recommended the board accept Mackay's resignation and thereby avoid any loyalty votes.

Immediately after his resignation, Mackay flew to London to meet Sir Max Aitken, Lord Beaverbrook's son and successor as university chancellor. When I met Mackay on his return in January, he told me that Sir Max had been furious at his resignation and had urged him to delay his retirement from the presidency by one year. B.L. "Bud" Jewett, a Fredericton doctor, formerly one of Beaverbrook's physicians and a member of the board, also went to meet Aitken. Mackay suspected that he had gone to England in order to get to Sir Max before Mackay did and to dissuade the chancellor from asking Mackay to withdraw his resignation. In telling me of Jewett's trip, Mackay complained about what a thorn Jewett had always been in his side.

In 2002 Mackay's friend Gordon Fairweather felt that Mackay had overstayed his welcome at UNB and that he should have resigned a few years earlier. He felt that Mackay had just "run out of steam" and that his resignation was a sad end.[27]

K.C. Irving, 1954.

Mackay's departure was indeed a sign that the university would be embarking on a new course after sixteen years of his frequently inspired presidential leadership.

While Louis Robichaud confessed surprise, and like Sir Max, asked Mackay to delay his resignation, he also indicated that "the fact that you had been in office in that capacity for a longer period than any other university president in Canada, had prepared me for such an eventual announcement."[28] Robichaud reported that his cabinet was unanimous in its belief that Mackay should remain in office for a further year, until the end of the 1969–70 academic year.

The Board of Governors met next on January 16. Jim Dineen, Desmond Pacey and Leslie Shemilt were proposed as candidates for the position of acting president. The board named Dineen as acting president-designate and then proceeded to select members for the Joint Nominating Committee for the appointment of a new president.[29] On March 12, Mackay wrote to Robichaud that, in line with the wishes of the government and those of Sir Max, he was prepared to remain as president "on a month-to-month basis until the end of the next academic year." The search for a successor had begun, and Mackay indicated that he would step down once his successor was announced and was available to serve.[30]

When Franz Martin returned to Fredericton after Christmas and found that Mackay had resigned, he noted in his journal, "We are all thrilled and jubilant to hear of Mackay's 'demise'. I like to think I may have had the tiniest bit to do with it."[31]

Chapter 7

THE BALLAD OF TOM MURPHY

Just before Christmas 1968, Tom Murphy woke up one morning to a report on CBC radio that he and John Oliver, as *Brunswickan* editor, were to be charged with contempt of court because of Murphy's December 3 "Spades Down" column, in which he claimed that the "courts of New Brunswick are the instruments of the corporate elite."

When he got over his initial surprise, Murphy's first reaction was to look for advice and support from friends Ann and Don Cameron, whom he had met through George Mossman of the Student Christian Movement. Don was a member of the English department, and Ann held a post-doctoral fellowship in psychology. Having recently moved to Fredericton, she had been distressed by the lack of progressive thinking and social action at UNB and feared what might happen to Murphy.[1] The Camerons invited him to a meeting with Duff Harper. Not looking directly at Murphy, the lawyer said: "If I were talking to Mr. Murphy, I would advise him to get out of here right away, because my understanding is that the Department of Justice has every intention of trying to prosecute between Christmas and New Year's and that they intend to play hardball." Murphy took his advice and left Fredericton, first to Sussex where he was put up by the daughter of the editor of the *King's County Record,* and then to an SCM conference in Winnipeg, not returning to Fredericton until the beginning of term in January, when he was served with the sheriff's papers.[2]

As editor of the *Brunswickan,* John Oliver had provided a relatively balanced coverage of events and opinions throughout the year, in spite of the fact that he had been caught up in the pressure and confusion of trying to report on the campus revolution. The staff of the *Brunswickan* were amateurs who had never been confronted with handling so much news at one time. Under these circumstances, Oliver felt Murphy was one of his more dependable contributors and had considerable confidence in his articles and his judgement. "Most of the time, I never read Tom's articles before they went in," Oliver reflected in 2002, and in reference to the "Spades Down" column, "I'm sure I didn't read that one before it went in."

Because he was Murphy's editor, however, Oliver was also charged with contempt of court. He was an economics student, and John Earl was one of his professors. Earl and Harold Sharp secured Duff Harper to act as Oliver's counsel, and Harper advised Oliver not to fight the case but to accept his guilt and apologize to the court. He took the heat, pleaded guilty, was fined $50.00 and was required to publish an apology. The apology was drafted by Harper and was laced with sarcasm to such an extent that Don Cameron later used it with his English classes as an example of satire.[3] A collection was taken in the courtroom, which paid Oliver's fine in cash on the spot.[4]

At the end of December 1968, John Paul Barry handed down his judgement in the case of the University of New Brunswick vs. Norman Strax. In this judgement, Barry found that Strax did indeed disrupt the university library and that he was "a promoter and organizer and an active participant in all of the incidents involved." He found "without hesitation" that Strax was legally suspended on September 24 and that "from the following day he was trespassing on the University premises." Barry did not feel that Mackay needed prior authorization from the Board of Governors to apply for the injunction, nor that the board had to approve the introduction of ID cards. Strax was completely responsible for the damages that he caused to the university, argued the judge. "The defendant embarked on a course of action designed to achieve certain objects and the fact that he chose certain methods is evidence that he himself was of the opinion that his methods would have such an effect on the administration that it would be forced to yield to his demands in order to conduct the normal operations of the institution." Barry felt that Strax had taken advantage of the liberal nature of the university. "The mere fact that the defendant was permitted to organize a group, hold a meeting in a university building and to distribute circulars containing such vulgar language and smearing personal attacks on responsible people is indicative of the licence (or abuse of freedom) allowed him. It was only when his conduct went to the extremes...that action was taken."

While Barry did not feel that there was a case for charging Strax for damages for which he was directly responsible, he did feel that, because Strax had acted "in a 'high-handed fashion' and persisted in ignoring the rights of others," there was a case to be made for awarding exemplary damages, and this he did, charging Strax two thousand dollars and costs.

Barry's conclusion was that the suspension of Strax was lawful and that there would be "an injunction restraining the defendant from returning to or entering upon any part of the lands and premises of the plaintiff and also restraining him from causing any nuisance or disturbance which would likely have the effect of disrupting the normal operations of the university."[5]

The UNB appeal to the courts meant that the university was not prepared to make any decisions or moves on the matter of Norman Strax while the matter was *sub judice*. In spite of the report of the McAllister Committee being available to the Board of Governors, even as late as the board meeting of December 19, the members of the board did not feel that it should be discussed or that any action should be taken until Barry had rendered his judgement.[6] With Barry's judgement at the end of December, it then became necessary to allow a month for the possible filing of an appeal. The Board of Governors only intended to take action on the Strax case at its February meeting at the earliest.[7]

The CAUT Academic Freedom and Tenure Committee was disturbed by what appeared to be deliberate delay at UNB and decided that it was time to play hardball by threatening UNB with censure if it would not deal with the Strax case. Alwyn Berland, who succeeded Percy Smith as CAUT executive secretary at the end of 1968, explained in 2000 that the CAUT had committed itself to a policy on academic freedom and tenure, "which was one of the real cornerstones of the establishment of the CAUT. It had now been flagrantly violated and we had to do something about it or we'd end up as paper tigers."[8]

The committee met on January 11, and on January 17 President Macpherson sent an ultimatum to Mackay. It had been fourteen weeks since James B. Milner had asked UNB to offer Strax an arbitration committee and eight weeks since that request had been confirmed by the CAUT Council, and yet UNB had still not acted. At this point, Macpherson upped the ante against UNB. Arbitration would no longer be sufficient, he wrote, since "the injunction which restrains Professor Strax from setting foot in the University in effect turns his suspension into a dismissal. To keep it in force now, while there has still been no adjudicative hearing of any charges arising out of the matters that made the suspension necessary, appears to be a denial of elementary justice." The lawsuit imposed on Strax by the university had also meant that Strax had incurred expenses, costs and "exemplary damages, which need not have been incurred if the University had granted an academic adjudicative hearing of charges against him."

If UNB wanted "to restore its standing in the academic community," Macpherson indicated that it would now have to take the following immediate steps:

> *(i) to institute arbitration proceedings along the lines of the CAUT policy statement in which arbitration of all claims by the university against Professor Strax and by Professor Strax against the university are submitted for settlement.*

> *(ii) to dissolve the injunction against Professor Strax; and*

> *(iii) to assume the entire costs of the litigation and to release Professor Strax from all liability for the damages and costs in your case against him.*

The Executive and the Finance Committee of CAUT would be meeting on February 8, and Macpherson warned that if he could not report that an adequate response had been made by the university to these proposals, he would have no choice but to recommend to the CAUT Council that the president and Board of Governors of the University of New Brunswick be censured.[9]

***

The summons Tom Murphy received on his return to Fredericton in January was in the form of a *Rule Nisi* requiring him to appear

*Chancellor Sir Max Aitken and Mackay with Senator Bobby Kennedy when he received his
UNB honorary degree at Fall Convocation 1967.*

before the Appeals Division of the Supreme Court of New
Brunswick to show cause why he should not be charged with
contempt of court. He was being held in contempt because his
Brunswickan article contained "certain comments, reflections and
innuendos" on the New Brunswick courts and on Mr. Justice
J. Paul Barry, which were "calculated to bring this Honourable
Court, Mr. Justice Barry and the proceedings in said trial into
public ridicule and contempt." Murphy was ordered to appear in
court on January 22, 1969.[10]

His first challenge was to find a lawyer to represent him. Duff
Harper had spent the better part of the fall representing Strax,
had just been representing Oliver and had been paid for neither
piece of work. He was not prepared to take on any more university cases. Murphy phoned a number of Fredericton lawyers, only
to find that no one would touch his case. He felt he was anathema

to the legal profession because of his association with Strax, but Ann Cameron felt the lawyers were afraid that their careers in New Brunswick could be destroyed if they took the case.[11]

Don Cameron suggested that Murphy try former Prime Minister John Diefenbaker, noted for his defence of civil rights. Murphy spoke to Diefenbaker, who was unable to take the case, since he was not practising at that time. He did authorize Murphy to use his name in court, however, which generated excited speculation in the local papers about the possibility of Diefenbaker appearing in Fredericton.

The Camerons and others, such as George Mossman, John Earl, Harold Sharp, Perry Robinson and Lawson Hunter, had no more luck in trying to find a lawyer. Eventually, the architect, Jon Oliver, suggested they see if they could interest the Canadian Civil Liberties Association (CCLA) in the case. In 1968 the CCLA had just recruited Alan Borovoy as its General Counsel, at the beginning of what would become a forty-one year career as one of the leading civil libertarians in Canada. Borovoy had earlier distinguished himself by taking up issues of racial discrimination in Ontario, poor government services for the First Nations and the cause of the Africville residents in Halifax. To everyone's relief, Borovoy agreed to take on Murphy's case. Because Borovoy was not a member of the New Brunswick Bar, he had to have a New Brunswick counsel of record, and Fredericton lawyer David Nicholson agreed to act in that capacity.[12]

I interviewed Alan Borovoy in Toronto in 2000 and we talked about Tom Murphy. Borovoy told me that when he first met Murphy, in order to give him confidence, he told him that he thought he had a wonderful name for a martyr and that, in years to come, he expected to hear people singing "The Ballad of Tom Murphy." In the context of the Strax Affair, Borovoy's comment is appropriate, since the trial of Tom Murphy deserves to be handed down in folk memory as evidence of the reaction of a terrified provincial society to student radicalism at a time before civil liberties were constitutionally protected through the *Canadian Charter of Rights and Freedoms*.

When Borovoy examined the case, he found that the provincial Department of Justice was using an "almost medieval procedure to nail somebody in the twentieth century." Under the "show cause" procedure, Murphy was assumed to be guilty and required to prove his innocence in court. The elderly prosecuting attorney, J.F.H. Teed of Saint John, had been called out of retirement because he had been involved in a similar trial when this procedure had last been invoked in New Brunswick many years before.[13]

The trial was held in the Supreme Court of New Brunswick before a judicial panel of three: Chief Justice G.F.G. Bridges, and Justices R.V. Limerick and Lou McC. Ritchie. Both Bridges and Ritchie were in their seventies, with Limerick only somewhat younger. Borovoy was intrigued by the trial and its context. "You had on the one hand," he said, "a prosecutor and the judges who all appeared to be at quite an advanced age, and then you had the kids at the university and in between you had the responsible parties." He developed a number of defence strategies, including one based on freedom of speech, with reference to the Diefenbaker *Bill of Rights*; one based on the argument that it was an anachronism from another era to argue that remarks made outside a court could "denigrate the court in the eyes of the community;" one that there was already a criminal code provision for contempt of court, even though it did not cover Murphy's case specifically; and one that argued that even though Murphy may have denigrated the courts, no one would have paid any attention to what he had to say.

To develop the latter argument, Borovoy sought to introduce sociological expertise into the court. Lynn McDonald, an assistant professor of sociology at McMaster University and a

Alan Borovoy, General Counsel of the Canadian Civil Liberties Association.

friend and former classmate of Ann Cameron, was invited by Borovoy to serve as an expert witness. She was to conduct a survey in the Fredericton community to determine the esteem in which the courts were held by those who had read Murphy's article as compared to those who had not. McDonald did not feel that Tom Murphy's comments about the corporate elite were at all outrageous for a sociologist and felt that they were an adequate reflection of the literature in the discipline. Nevertheless, in order to help with Murphy's defence, she conducted her survey as requested.[14]

"I'm sure you'll be shocked to hear," Borovoy told me in 2000, that McDonald "found no distinction between the two groups of people." The judges, however, were upset at the idea of sociological evidence and ruled that the study was inadmissible because it was based on hearsay, since McDonald was only drawing conclusions from what people had told her. McDonald left

Fredericton without presenting the results of her survey. She was appalled by the court and the proceedings against Tom Murphy. She thought the judges "were ignorant, out of date and close minded in not knowing what sociology was."[15]

In fact, the argument that most interested the judges was Borovoy's suggestion that they had no jurisdiction to hear the case because the *Criminal Code* provided avenues of appeal, while the case had been brought in the first instance to the New Brunswick Court of Appeal, thereby depriving the accused of one of the normal avenues of appeal to which the *Criminal Code* entitled him. Appeal in this case could only be to the Supreme Court of Canada.

At any rate, the judges dismissed all of Borovoy's arguments and convicted Murphy. In discussion on sentence, Teed argued for a jail penalty on the grounds that "the organization" which had paid to bring Borovoy to Fredericton would pay any fine for Murphy. In response, Borovoy read off a list of the people on the letterhead of the Canadian Civil Liberties Association — Pierre Berton, June Callwood, Barbara Frum, Robert Fulford — and said, "Quite an imposing array of subversives, my Lords."

When I asked Borovoy why he thought Murphy had been charged as he had been, Borovoy said his impression was "that Strax scared the hell out of the establishment in the community." People in Fredericton had read about the kind of disruptive behaviour that Strax practiced but had never actually seen it in New Brunswick. They were really afraid, and it just played to their authoritarian instincts. Borovoy, in fact, found himself in the middle of the issue: "I had problems with the old guard because of their conservatism, and I had problems with Strax and his followers because of their 'infantile leftism.' I thought that in some ways both extremes were deserving of each other, except the kids were younger and that's more forgivable in young people than it is in older people." In those days, Borovoy said, "I tried my best to put across to young people that you don't have to choose between reactionary conservatism on one hand and foolish leftism on the other." He attributed the setting up of a Fredericton chapter of the Canadian Civil Liberties Association shortly afterwards as an attempt to provide young people with a centrist course of action. At the time, Borovoy felt that this case offered dangerous precedents for the future, but the provisions of the *Canadian Charter of Rights and Freedoms* of the 1980s meant that such a procedure could never again be used."[16]

***

Mackay's disdain for student participation in the university became apparent in another issue dealt with by the SRC under Alastair Robertson. The question of student representation on the University Senate was a matter which had to be resolved subsequent to the 1968 *University Act.* A joint committee of four faculty members, including myself, named by the Senate, and four students, named by the SRC, began its work in November 1968. It was a good committee, discussions moved smoothly, there was common agreement on the need for student representation and recommendations were easily developed. A report was ready by early February 1969, which recommended that seven student representatives from Fredericton and one from Saint John should be directly elected to the Senate by the students and that henceforth all meetings of senate should be open. The report was to be presented to both the Senate and the SRC for approval.

When Alastair Robertson, as acting SRC president, met Mackay to discuss the report, however, he found that the president had many reservations about it. "The Senate was most unsure on the question," said Mackay. "There was little likelihood of an early settlement; many members did not want any students at all." Robertson commented that, "the more he talked, the further the prospect receded." On Sunday, February 16, Mackay summoned the faculty members of the joint committee to his office. George McAllister was also present, but the student members of the committee were not invited. At that meeting, Mackay indicated his dissatisfaction with the recommendations on student representation and suggested strongly to the faculty members that they change the recommendations. I was one of the faculty members present and was disgusted with the kind of pressure that Mackay was putting on the committee, as were the other faculty members. The committee had worked smoothly and well up to this point, with responsible and co-operative student members. After the meeting, I met Robertson in MacKenzie House and told him about the meeting in Mackay's office.

That was the last straw for Robertson. He submitted his resignation as acting president at the SRC meeting that evening[17] and followed it with a blistering and widely distributed public statement in which he explained that he had resigned because he could "no longer do business with a man, and men, to whom the normal courtesies of negotiation mean little or nothing, to whom the SRC is something to be used when convenient, and humoured the rest of the time, that urge their concern for student representation on the Senate when it is convenient, and dismiss it airily when it might be awkward; that talk of an open attitude to student aspirations in the one breath, and in the next treat them with the arrogance of a Roman emperor." The president and the university administration did not accept the SRC's right to a bargaining position, "and they consequently do not feel any need to preserve the amenities of negotiation."[18]

Robertson's resignation statement was the last flourish from the outgoing council. Neither Mackay and the senior administration, nor many of the students were sorry to see the end of this particular council, which had managed to stage a public humiliation of Mackay and his deans and had then gone on to try to use student funds to pay the court costs of student radicals. The issue of student representation on the Senate was settled in the spring of 1969 when the Senate and the SRC approved the recommendations of the joint committee, which had not been altered as the president had asked.

In many ways, the ventures into the courts were incidental to the Strax Affair. The injunction against Strax was designed to keep him from stirring up further problems on campus while the university considered how his case should be disposed of through university channels. The charge against Tom Murphy, and in particular, his trial before the Supreme Court of New Brunswick was a bizarre and quasi-medieval exercise by the community at large to control the potential challenge of student radicalism to the stability of New Brunswick traditional institutions.

Chapter 8
THE ROAD TO CENSURE

On February 8 the CAUT Executive and Finance Committee called a special meeting of the CAUT Council for March 15 in the Airport Hilton Hotel in Montreal to discuss the situation at UNB, and if necessary, "to censure the president and board of the University of New Brunswick." As defined by the CAUT, censure meant "that all members of the CAUT outside the University of New Brunswick would be advised not to accept appointments there and others considering appointments there would be advised to inform themselves of the CAUT reasons for the censure."[1] The CAUT Council had imposed censure for the first time in May 1968, on the president and the Board of Governors of Simon Fraser University.[2]

CAUT President Macpherson, along with James B. Milner, the chair of the Academic Freedom and Tenure Committee, and Executive Secretary Berland, visited Fredericton late in February. They attended a meeting of the AUNBT, where Berland sensed a great deal of hostility, most of it questioning the right of the CAUT to tell the university how to run its own affairs. The faculty was obviously divided, and Berland was surprised by how much hatred Strax had generated.[3]

The delegation met the UNB board on February 20, when Macpherson continually stressed that the CAUT wanted the injunction lifted because it might become a precedent for the way universities deal with difficult faculty members in the future. If the injunction were lifted and Strax were given an arbitration committee, Macpherson assured the board that the CAUT would not defend Strax should he then engage in disruptive action on campus. One member of the board zeroed in on the differences between the CAUT and the AUNBT, asking Doug Brewer if the CAUT Policy Statement on Academic Freedom and Tenure was being followed by the AUNBT. Brewer replied that the AUNBT had passed a motion in support of arbitration, but had not expressed any opinion on lifting the injunction or covering costs. Macpherson was then asked if UNB would be censured if the board decision satisfied the procedures of the AUNBT but not those of the CAUT. Macpherson replied that the views of the AUNBT would be respected by the CAUT Council but, at the same time, the council might still feel it had to go ahead with censure. After the visitors left, the board supported the AUNBT position but not the one taken by the CAUT. It agreed to a non-binding arbitration of certain matters of redress connected with the suspension of Strax but refused to apply to dissolve the injunction or to assume Strax's court costs.[4]

In January Strax had sought the advice of the Academic Freedom and Tenure Committee about whether he should appeal the Barry decision in the courts. The committee had been opposed to Strax appealing the decision, which would delay matters with UNB, and when Strax decided to go ahead with an appeal in late February,[5] Mackay immediately informed Macpherson that "the board could undertake no step which could be construed as prejudicing or compromising Professor Strax's right to an appeal."[6] Macpherson was convinced the lawsuit was being used to justify inaction, since the university could have stopped it at any time by agreement with Strax. "This is the really serious matter that the CAUT is bound to resist," argued Macpherson. "If it is not challenged, this use of the injunction and civil suits could become a pattern for any Canadian university that wished to delay a proper adjudicative hearing until it was too late to afford the individual any justice."[7] Mackay retorted: "In effect, your position would appear to be that a university should never resort to the processes of the law, and if it does it will incur censure. Surely, this position is indefensible in principle and a censure in the present circumstances, is unwarranted."[8] Such was the state of debate between Macpherson and Mackay on the eve of the CAUT Council meeting of March 15.

While this debate continued, there remained the question of the actual employment status of Strax. Bill Argue, the dean of science, sought advice on the status of Strax's employment contract. The university solicitor pointed out that, while there was no formal contract, there had been an exchange of letters in 1968 that extended Strax's probationary appointment to June 30, 1969, for which he was still being paid even though he was suspended. Since Strax was on a probationary appointment, the solicitor felt that he was entitled to receive reasonable notice prior to June 30, 1969, if his probationary appointment was not to be continued.[9] Argue passed this advice along to Mackay, who in turn arranged for Boone to remind Strax that his contract with UNB would expire on June 30.[10]

Unable to formulate a coherent position because of its internal divisions, the AUNBT was losing whatever initiative it had as the CAUT increased its pressure on Mackay and the board. By the time the AUNBT membership met again on February 7, the CAUT executive, without consultation with the AUNBT, had sent its ultimatum to Mackay. Caught between the CAUT and the UNB administration, the AUNBT tried to define its position in the conflict. The best that it could achieve on February 7 was to pass a weak motion "that this meeting of the AUNBT supports the efforts of CAUT to persuade the Board of Governors to comply with our resolution of November 26th."[11]

A few days later, Brewer, who had been working to hold the AUNBT together, explained the AUNBT reaction to the CAUT demands in a letter to Percy Smith. Some members, Brewer wrote, "did not like the two conditions of the injunction and the costs being included as a prerequisite for settlement." He also explained his own position on the matter: "My main concern in this whole matter has been to attempt to have instituted a proper adjudicative procedure which will ensure any faculty member a fair hearing and settlement. I do not agree with the inclusion of the removal of the injunction and the assumption of legal and court costs by the university as prior conditions, but rather as matters for the arbitration committee to decide upon. This opinion is shared by a large segment of my executive."[12]

When the AUNBT executive met at the end of February, it supported the gesture of the board toward arbitration, and in separate motions urged both the CAUT and Mackay to get arbitration started immediately. Seven members of the executive had been present at the meeting, including Murray Young and Les Shemilt, who were also members of the Board of Governors. Both motions passed by six votes in favour, none opposed and one abstention.[13] Vice-President Perry Robinson had not attended the executive meeting and insisted that Brewer make his absence known to the CAUT and to Mackay and "that had he been there, he would have voted against such action."[14]

When Percy Smith wrote that he had difficulty reconciling the AUNBT motions with the November 26 motion of the AUNBT,[15] Brewer explained that the February 28 motions were intended to encourage the move toward setting up arbitration for Strax and were "meant as a positive move to having the problem settled." While appreciating the point that the CAUT was trying to make in connection with the injunction, the AUNBT executive did not feel that it could comment on this because it had not yet had any instructions from its membership.

On March 6, Doug Brewer resigned the presidency of the AUNBT. In a letter to the membership he said that the CAUT censure was very likely to come about because the CAUT was standing firm on the issues of the injunction and the costs. "Because my personal feelings are mixed on these issues," he wrote, "I cannot support the CAUT censure motion on these issues alone, in view of the board's acceptance of the principle of arbitration. I have found myself caught (again) between the national policies of the CAUT, and what is attainable at this institution. I am convinced that my usefulness as your president is now nil, and I am very frustrated with the whole business."[16] As his parting gesture, Brewer called a general meeting of the membership for Sunday, March 8.

Issues came to a head for the AUNBT at this March 8 meeting when the deep splits within the faculty became apparent to all. Ninety-nine people attended the meeting and Harold Sharp led off by questioning the right of the executive to send its motions to the CAUT and to Mackay. Since two members of the board had attended the executive meeting, Sharp asked if Strax or his representatives had also been invited to attend. Nevertheless, a motion supporting the executive and its action was carried by a narrow margin.

Don Cameron and Sharp then proposed "that the Board of Governor's offer to submit the Strax case only to non-binding arbitration was unsatisfactory," which was defeated, with thirty-five people voting for the motion, thirty-nine voting against and fourteen abstaining. Another motion by Cameron and Sharp "that the AUNBT support the position taken by the CAUT executive in the Strax case" was also defeated, twenty-seven voting in favour, forty-three against and eighteen abstaining. Another motion "that we support the aims of CAUT but cannot support the action of CAUT executive in the implementation of its policy with regard to the Strax case and that we urge the CAUT executive to keep in close communications with AUNBT," passed by "a large majority" with only one abstention. When a motion to adjourn was defeated thirty-two to thirty-five, Harold Sharp introduced an ironic motion:

> ...*that the membership of the AUNBT commends the faculty members on the Board of Governors for their unfaltering support of the position taken by the administration and the other members of the board. We also commend the faculty members on the Board of Governors on their consistent stand on the matters of academic due process. We fully support the position they have taken in dealing with Professor Strax and trust that future situations of this type will continue to be handled in a fashion that will prove equally satisfactory to the university.*[17] This motion, in turn, was defeated.

The following day, Perry Robinson, now acting president of the AUNBT, sent a letter to Mackay urging him "to take what action is still open to you to avoid the possibility of censure to the University of New Brunswick."[18]

***

The judgement in the Queen vs. Thomas Raymond Murphy was handed down on March 12, when Chief Justice Bridges wrote, on behalf of the three judges:

Doug Brewer, President of the AUNBT, 1968–69.

There is...a limit to what a person may say or write of a judge or court. In my opinion, the defendant exceeded that limit in his malignment of Mr. Justice Barry. He was not even satisfied with that but proceeded to make a most uncalled for attack on the integrity of the courts of New Brunswick. I have no hesitation in holding the article was calculated to bring Mr. Justice Barry and the courts of New Brunswick into contempt. The defendant must be found guilty.[19]

Murphy was sentenced to ten days in jail, with one day off for good behaviour, and was not fined. The judges refused to suspend the imposition of sentence to allow Borovoy to prepare a notice of appeal to the Supreme Court of Canada, although Murphy and Borovoy had already agreed they would only appeal if the jail term were more than thirty days. Murphy had been worried about being hit with a huge fine because he had no money at all.

He served his time in the York County Jail in Fredericton and was released on March 20, the day of the major student demonstration at UNB. While he joined the demonstration for some time, he was really finished with activism in Fredericton. He tried to write some exams at the end of term, but was prevented from doing so in a couple of cases because he had missed too many classes. Then he left Fredericton and moved to Toronto, where he took up his position as the national president of the SCM for the following year.[20]

At one point the SRC planned to use student money to assist Oliver and Murphy with their court costs. At its meeting of January 26, 1969, the SRC passed a motion to give Oliver and Murphy financial aid to help them with their legal expenses.[21] The Engineering Undergraduate Society and the Forestry Association did not feel this was an appropriate use of student monies, however, and presented a petition signed by 991 individuals objecting to legal aid for Oliver and Murphy.[22] The SRC backed away from the issue completely on February 23, however, and rescinded the original motion to provide legal aid to Oliver and Murphy.[23] There the matter rested as far as the SRC was concerned.

Meanwhile Duff Harper was having difficulty collecting his money. In January, he sent Harold Sharp an invoice for the costs connected with defending John Oliver.[24] In early February Harper wrote to C.B. Macpherson, the president of the CAUT, pointing out that when Vincent Kelly first arrived in Saint John to defend Strax, he assured Harper that the CAUT had guaranteed "at least the first two days of his fees and expenses, as well as mine." Harper had instituted legal action against Strax and felt there had been a breach of faith in his relationship with the CAUT. "I do not pretend to understand either the present generation nor the aims and objects of your Association, but in my naivety I have jeopardized my professional career, devoted a great deal of time in research and alienated my relations with

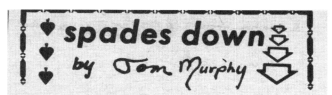

A short while ago, I testified in the Supreme Court of New Brunswick on the Strax case. That court was a mockery of justice. I, along with any of the other defence witnesses, might well have testified to the bottle-throwing mob that on several occasions gathered outside the window of Liberation 130. The treatment would be about the same. Bill Walker's geology pick was Judge Barry's gavel in court. The intent was the same.

Take for instance the attitudes of Judge Barry. I am in no position to accuse a man of being biased; his manners have been self-convicting. Defence counsel was constantly asked to delete or at least rephrase their questions. This request was inevitably accompanied by a recitation of the rules of court, long enough to be inhibiting. The crown, of course, was not subjected to this same sort of treatment.

But this is minor compared to the manner in which Vince Kelly, one of Dr. Strax's lawyers was dismissed.

***

Just before we had entered the courtroom, Kelly was talking to us (several defence witnesses) about the testimony that we had to offer. The judge's secretary walked by. Kelly, after receiving her approval, asked her if she would contact Miss Gertrude Gunn, chief librarian, asking her if she could come down and testify. *No mention, whatsoever, was made of a court order from the judge. There are four witnesses to this fact.*

When Miss Gunn, obviously upset, took her place on the witness stand (just after I had finished), she explained her presence to the judge by saying that she had received a court order issued by him through his secretary. Judge Barry called an immediate recess to clarify the situation. How one can clarify the situation without talking to all parties involved is beyond me — but at any rate, the judge refused to talk to Mr. Kelly.

When court reconvened, Barry immediately told Harper that Kelly was dismissed from the case. Kelly attempted to inject an element of truth into the courtroom, but Barry cut him off before he had a chance to be heard. I am sorry to say this, but either Judge Barry, his secretary, or Miss Gertrude Gunn was mistaken. These are the cold facts. There are no other options.

* * *

The courts in New Brunswick are simply the instruments of the corporate elite. Their duty is not so much to make *just* decisions as to make *right* decisions (i.e. decisions which will further perpetuate the elite which controls and rewards them.) Court appointments are political appointments. Only the naive would reject the notion that an individual becomes a justice or judge after he proves his worth to the establishment.

Tom Murphy's offending Brunswickan *column of December 3, 1968*

the Bench in an effort to do an honest, decent and proper job."
Harper reminded Macpherson that for all this time, Strax was on
full salary with UNB and Harper hoped that "the milk of human
kindness is to be found in the heart of the CAUT and that your
organization will not repudiate its moral obligations to the legal
profession."[25] Some months later the CAUT covered a portion of
Harper's costs.

The AUNBT executive chose Perry Robinson and chemist
Israel Unger as its representatives to the special CAUT Council
meeting in Montreal on March 15.[26] Other members of the executive asked Robinson to include Desmond Pacey as a member
of the official AUNBT delegation to the council meeting, since,
as secretary to the faculty, he could speak on behalf of the whole
faculty of UNB.[27]

On March 13, historian Jim Chapman participated in a teach-
in, where he gave a public explanation of the rift between the
AUNBT and the CAUT as he saw it: "AUNBT's position on the
Strax case remains what it has been from the beginning: support
for the principle of arbitration." Because of the importance that
the AUNBT placed on arbitration, "it is critical of the CAUT
executive's insistence on lifting the injunction against Dr. Strax
before arbitration can be entered into. In other words, the CAUT
executive is saying: 'We won't start peace negotiations until the
bombing stops.' The majority of AUNBT believes that the manner in which the CAUT executive has handled the Strax case,
namely by press release, open telegrams and ultimatums is not
one calculated to aid in settlement of a dispute." The CAUT
should get on with setting up the arbitration and not divert the
issue by the imposition of censure. "AUNBT stands for arbitration with or without the lifting of the injunction."[28]

Historian Dick Wilbur, in a CBC radio talk on March 14, put
the case for faculty unionization. He argued that "it's about time
university professors swallowed their pride, forgot their status and

formed unions." Wilbur said that the UNB faculty were divided over the Strax Affair. There were "those supporting the president's actions, the inevitable middle group refusing to take sides, and a vociferous minority working for Strax's reinstatement," and in close touch with the CAUT. The latter group included professors Sharp, Earl and Robinson. Wilbur concluded that "one thing this prolonged and acrimonious UNB dispute has done is to acquaint many academics with the plain fact that they are employees with little say over tenure, salary and promotions. Very few bona fide union locals would have to admit to that these days."[29]

The developments at UNB were well known throughout the Canadian academic community. When the university's student History Club organized a conference on Maritime studies in January or February, 1969, the two invited guests, George Rawlyk, from Queens and Michael Cross from the University of Toronto, refused to attend any conference to be held on the UNB campus because the university was in dispute with CAUT. The History Club executive arranged for the conference to be held instead on the adjacent campus of St. Thomas University. Professors Rawlyk and Cross arrived in Fredericton with much publicity but to a rather cool welcome from the members of the UNB history department, who felt the visitors had imposed an unnecessary burden on the student organizers.

The CAUT Council met at the Airport Hilton in Montreal on Saturday, March 15. There were forty voting delegates. Thirty-one universities were represented by the heads of their faculty associations. Perry Robinson was the main delegate from UNB, George McAllister was there in his capacity as vice-president of the CAUT and Desmond Pacey as the secretary to the faculty. The motion placed before the council read:

I. That this council censure the president and the Board of Governors of the University of New

Brunswick for suspending a faculty member from all rights and privileges in the university without stating charges against him and providing for an academic adjudicative hearing, and for resorting to and maintaining an injunction and a civil lawsuit on limited issues without first providing for an academic adjudicative hearing, and using the existence of that lawsuit as a reason for preventing any full academic adjudicative hearing on all issues.

II. That the censure of the president and the Board of Governors of the University of New Brunswick take the following form:

(i) Immediate public release of the text of the motion of censure.

(ii) Publication in the next issue of the Bulletin of a detailed account of a history of the Strax case, and of steps leading to censure.

(iii) Publication in the Bulletin of the recommendation that members of CAUT should not accept employment at UNB at the present time.

(iv) Notification to other faculty associations (e.g. AAUP, AUT, etc.) of these actions with recommendations that their members request further information from CAUT before accepting employment at UNB

(v) Publication of advertisements of these actions in leading education and professional journals in

Canada, the Commonwealth and the United States.

III. That the Executive and Finance Committee be empowered to administer items iii, iv and v above in the light of further developments and be instructed to report its actions to the next council meeting.

Robinson and Pacey both spoke, warning that the imposition of censure on UNB would split the faculty and could do irreparable damage to the effectiveness of the AUNBT. The question was put at 4:20 pm and the motion for censure was carried, with thirty-six voting in favour, three against and one person abstaining.[30]

Chapter 9
CENSURED!

In addition to giving the official student leadership some focus and direction, the CAUT censure also brought the faculty together. In a CBC radio commentary, Don Cameron was amazed at the way that the censure of UNB had served to create this unity. Prior to the CAUT Council meeting, there had been bitter divisions. "UNB is a very conservative school in a very conservative province, and the faculty has been deeply divided between distaste for Dr. Strax and distaste for the university's reaction." Yet, after censure, "instead of amplifying, our discords seem to have had a therapeutic effect that no one had even dreamed of…I'm stunned to report that censure — far from disruption — has brought the first feeling of unity in months."[1]

The CAUT censure also created a degree of unity among UNB students. The annual elections for a new student council had been scheduled for February 26. Because the out-going council had been so radical, many students had felt disenfranchised and excluded and were now determined to elect a more conservative and responsive council. This was particularly the feeling among the engineering students who had initially opposed proposals to pay the court costs of Oliver and Murphy and were now determined to get the kind of student council they could support.

The result was the installation of a more conservative SRC on March 2 under the presidency of Michael Start. Start was a third-year arts student from Fredericton, whose father, Doug Start, was the UNB director of music and whose mother was a secretary in the chemistry department. In the early 1960s Michael had been a member of my Scout troop, and at that time had been a close friend of Tom Murphy, although their paths had diverged by the time they reached university. Start was a quiet and serious individual, the kind of person one might describe as a "straight arrow." He had earlier been a supporter of the Mobilization and had helped in the organization of the 1967 trip to Washington, although, because he was also a member of the Naval Reserves, he had not gone on the trip. He had served on the SRC under Wayne Beach and had been second vice-president to David Cox.

Start was not comfortable with the polarization of the students during the winter of 1968–69. He was a good friend of Don Lutes, the president of the Engineering Undergraduate Society, who felt that Strax and his followers were upsetting the kind of university that he had chosen to attend. When Start agreed to run for the SRC presidency, he knew that he would have the support of the engineers, and he deliberately ran a conservative campaign designed to "restore peace to the family" and show "fairness to all," reaching out to those students who had felt disenfranchised. In deciding to run for the presidency, Start had been encouraged by Eric Garland, a popular civil engineering professor who was also a member of the Board of Governors. Start recalled in 2000 that Garland was always in the background during the election campaign and sought to influence the direction of events from the sidelines. Start won the election against two other candidates, feeling he had been chosen because he represented the "least of three evils." Robert Hess, the most radical of the candidates, finished bottom of the poll.

Start and his council had to immediately go into defensive mode, since events in the university were running outside their control. The first eighteen days of Start's presidency were the most intense as he entered the maelstrom of the politics of the Strax Affair. The rest of his term as president was anticlimactic.[2] Nevertheless, the Start SRC dealt effectively with the situation, determined as it was to hold the student body together and to reflect the student interest to the administration, the board and the wider community. Start worked closely with members of his council to fashion a strategy for the SRC in the middle of the campus crisis. Above all, they refused to take a position either for or against Strax. For them, as for many other students, the issue now became how much impact the CAUT censure of UNB would have on the quality and acceptability of University of New Brunswick degrees. A number of students claimed to fear that their degrees would now not be worth the money they had been spending.[3]

The first action of the new council was to ensure that students were aware of the arguments of the different parties to the dispute and to outline the potential significance of UNB being placed under censure by the CAUT, using the campus media. A broadly based public relations campaign followed, coordinated by a small committee of council.[4] The theme of this public relations campaign was summed up in a telegram from Start to Premier Robichaud, indicating that "the likely effect of censureship will be a deterioration of the quality of education offered here. We feel that neither the principle of administrative autonomy nor the principle of academic freedom are as important as the principle of the best possible education for the students." The matter was brought up in the provincial legislature, when, in reply to a question by opposition leader Richard Hatfield, Robichaud said "he fully supports the stand taken by the students and added he trusted 'the full legislature will stand behind this stand taken by the Student Representative Council.'"

While Start and his council were finding their way, the Mobilization SDS was still active, but not very effective. It had resumed its meetings at the end of January and was meeting on a weekly basis through February and early March, trying to decide where it should strike next. In early February, it planned to stage an event, such as an invasion of that month's board meeting or the occupation of Mackay's office to coincide with the meeting. The only problem was that it thought the board would be meeting on February 5, when it actually met on February 8. With a mistake like that, enthusiasm readily fizzled. On February 13 the Mobilization SDS successfully hosted a campus visit by Karl Wolff, the president of the German SDS, who was touring North America to raise money for the German SDS defence fund.[5] An attempt to reoccupy Liberation 130 on February 17, however, was a disastrous failure. In his journal, Franz Martin explains the divisions in the SDS between those, like Martin, who wanted to develop careful strategy, and those he called the "action freaks," led by John Robinson and Clayton Burns, who fancied themselves the "revolutionary vanguard" and would do anything. The reoccupation was planned for February 18, but at the planning meeting on February 17, Mobilization SDS decided to act immediately. About nine people got into Strax's former office that evening, but the room was surrounded by the Fredericton City Police and they were ordered to leave.[6]

For the March 18 general meeting of the AUNBT, the executive sought to generate a degree of consensus in the organization by carefully crafting a motion to reflect differing viewpoints, while calling on the board to do everything in its power to satisfy the conditions for the removal of censure. The board was asked to:

> i) *Invite Professor Strax to enter into negotiations with the board concerning his situation vis-à-vis the university; and on condition that he will*

state his election of arbitration in accordance with procedures endorsed by the CAUT, abandon his present appeal to the court, and that he will give his word that he will not engage in (nor encourage others to engage in) activities that might precipitate legal procedures against him while the arbitration procedures are being decided, make application to have the injunction against him dissolved.

ii) Establish an arbitration committee, mutually acceptable to Professor Strax and the board, to enter immediately into inquiries and deliberations relating to the issues of controversy.

iii) Notify the Executive and Finance Committee of the Canadian Association of University Teachers as soon as conditions of item (i) have been agreed upon by both parties and request that they participate in future negotiations and procedures of arbitration when called upon by either, or both, parties.

The motion was strongly supported at the meeting, passing by a vote of ninety in favour, six opposed and with only twenty-two abstentions. The executive was congratulated by Desmond Pacey on fashioning a motion that received such a large vote of approval.[7]

Reactions to the censure from the broader community were mixed. Federal Justice Minister John Turner expressed regrets to Mackay that the censure vote had gone against UNB.[8] Murray Sargeant, the Fredericton superintendent of schools, wrote that "teaching bodies with which I was affiliated" had in the past censured school boards, but these boards "received just as many applications as before, no teachers left because of the censure and everything went along as before."[9] Louise Pinet, the president of the New Brunswick Union of Students, wrote to Robichaud on behalf of the Union on March 17, asking him and his government to bring "the two parties involved together to resolve this educational crisis."[10]

Mackay received support from the *Moncton Transcript*. The whole matter, argued the *Transcript*, "hinges around the rights of the employer. Has the university not got the right to fire — just as it has the right to hire? Are the only rights and freedoms those of radical students and radical teachers? The action of CAUT," the editorial concluded, "is symptomatic of a sickness which seems to have infected all too many people today. It is a disease that apparently seeks to spread distrust of all established order."

High-school teachers from Moncton picked up on the *Transcript* editorial. On April 1, thirty-six teachers from Harrison Trimble High School, including a future chair of UNB's Board of Governors, Ilsa Greenblatt, sent support to the president, faculty and administration of UNB for holding "the line against student unrest. If you fail at the university level to contain student unrest, it may become much more of a problem in the high school where even fewer students have reached mental maturity."[11]

Once the censure was in place, C.B. Macpherson of the CAUT sought to encourage UNB to come to a quick settlement, telling Mackay immediately that the CAUT executive had been given discretion not to proceed with all the penalties of the censure if the Board of Governors should act rapidly. Specifically, Macpherson indicated that "we are content to leave the matter of costs and damages to the board's decision after arbitration, and to accept a morally binding arbitration, but the council is uncompromising about the injunction."[12]

The Board of Governors was scheduled to meet on March 20 to deal with the CAUT censure. Macpherson's letter helped encourage negotiations with UNB, so that, when Premier Robichaud wrote to Mackay on the eve of the meeting and offered the services of an independent mediator,[13] he received his answer from Macpherson, who phoned the premier to indicate that the appointment of a mediator now "could only delay settlement of the dispute and would not serve the interest of the students." Macpherson assured Robichaud "that the Board of Governors and CAUT appear very close to agreement."[14]

The reaction of UNB students to the censure had been measured and effective and earned Mike Start and his council considerable credit as balanced players in this crisis. The council held its regular meeting on Sunday, March 16, the day after the censure. To demonstrate student concern about its impact, the executive presented a plan for a student strike and a peaceful demonstration outside the board meeting on March 20. In order to maintain control over the demonstration, the SRC set up a coordinating committee to plan and direct that event.[15] The *Brunswickan* put out a special issue explaining and emphasizing the nature of the penalty that censure imposed on the university and a special mass meeting was held in the ballroom of the Student Union Building. On the panel at the meeting, Les Shemilt, representing the board, was harangued by Lawson Hunter at his most demagogic. Political positions were being defined, and Hunter felt it was important to discredit Shemilt, one of the liberal members of the board. Posters were painted and sound trucks were hired for Thursday, March 20. On March 18 Start informed Mackay of the planned demonstration and at the same time assured him this demonstration would be "peaceful and well organized" and that it should be seen as "purely a statement of concern by the majority of the students."[16]

With the CAUT censure, the Mobilization SDS wanted to do something itself in connection with the March 20 board meeting, but there was no consensus within that group on what they could do. Eventually, they decided to work with the SRC in preparing for the demonstration. Franz Martin and others made signs and posters, but Martin's comment in his journal on March 20 was that "the SDS was eager but incoherent; the SRC panicky over the SDS."[17]

One of the annual events in the UNB calendar had been the celebration of Founder's Day, which was scheduled in 1969 for March 20, the same day as the meeting of the Board of Governors. This celebration, which had been devised by Colin Mackay when he was an undergraduate in the 1940s, involved inviting a prominent speaker to campus to participate in an evening ceremony in Memorial Hall, when the university paid its "quit rent" to the Lieutenant-Governor, following which the speaker delivered an address. It was a formal ceremony and included the wearing of academic robes, and in more recent years a procession of the University Senate. Traditionally, the afternoon had been given over to a panel discussion, when the invited speaker would discuss a topic of current concern with UNB students and faculty. One year, Tommy Douglas, then leader of the New Democratic Party, had been the speaker and the panel had been on the topic of health care.

The panel discussion was normally organized by the Corona Society, the student honour society, consisting of students selected for the excellence of their academic achievement and their extra-curricular involvement. In 1969 the Corona Society proposed to designate the panel discussion as a "teach-in" on the topic: "The Critical University: A Criticism from Within." The featured guest for Founders' Day 1969 was to be Claude Bissell, the President of the University of Toronto, and the Corona Society had invited Martin Loney, the leading student radical at Simon Fraser University and president-elect of the Canadian Union of Students, to be the visiting student on the panel. The SRC and the administration were asked to support Loney's visit financially but, when Mackay and Pacey learned of this plan to confront Bissell with Loney in the midst of the crisis over the

UNB censure, they pulled the plug and cancelled Founder's Day. It was not celebrated again for a good number of years.[18]

On March 20, the Board of Governors met in the Old Arts Building, with the CAUT censure as the most important item on their agenda. In the morning, the meeting received delegations from the SRC, the Faculties of Arts and Science, the AUNBT and the University Senate. After lunch, the board passed the following motion, which effectively accepted the conditions laid down by the CAUT by agreeing:

> *1. To an arbitration to be considered morally persuasive and binding with respect to the disciplinary action appropriate to the circumstances present to the suspension of Professor Strax;*
>
> *2. To an application being made to dissolve or vacate the injunction simultaneously on agreement reached as to the terms of the submission to arbitration, the procedures and constitution of the arbitration tribunal;*
>
> *3. To continue to defer enforcement of costs and damages arising on the litigation pending the outcome of the arbitration and to consider matters of costs and damages subsequent to and on the outcome of the arbitration;*
>
> *4. To endeavour, on the outcome of the arbitration, to effect a settlement in full of all issues present to the litigation.*

This motion was contingent on the Executive and Finance Committee of the CAUT simultaneously agreeing to recommend to the CAUT Council that the censure resolution against UNB be removed. Should the CAUT not accept this proposal, the board was prepared to accept mediation as proposed by Premier Robichaud. It also agreed that appropriate procedures should be adopted to govern future cases of suspension and dismissal.

When asked in 2000 why the board had accepted the CAUT terms, Les Shemilt remembered that many members of the board, especially the faculty members, felt that the CAUT terms were moderate and reasonable and that there had been too much emphasis already on legal activity, such as the imposition of the injunction. It was also apparent to many members of the board that the CAUT was concerned about the long-term impact of the censure and wanted a resolution as soon as possible.[19]

At the end of the meeting, Perry Robinson and Mike Start were told of the board's decision. Robinson was encouraged and felt that the CAUT would be willing to lift censure once the university had acted as intended. Mike Start indicated that the students would like to hear an explanation of the board decision, and Mackay agreed to attend a student meeting that evening.[20]

The board meeting had taken place against a backdrop of student demonstration. The board room in the Old Arts Building, the "oldest university building in Canada," was on the second floor. The rest of the building housed the administrative offices of the president, vice-presidents and the registrar, while the Faculty Club occupied the top floor. The building had been built in 1828, and for many years in the nineteenth century had housed the whole university.

In spite of Start's assurance to Mackay that the demonstration would be peaceful and well-controlled, there was always the danger that things might get out of hand. With the possibility of the occupation of buildings or offices, or the burning of buildings and destruction of property, the university had taken precautions. For the March demonstration, the security police on campus

Protestors with a coffin representing the UNB Board of Governors, March 20, 1969.

were removed from Barnett's direction and put under the com-
mand of Brigadier A.F.B. Knight. Knight, a retired soldier, was
the university's director of personnel, and was responsible for
monitoring the demonstration and the reaction of the security
police. His plan was to allow the demonstration to run its course,
provided no attempt was made to occupy the Old Arts Building
or any other building on campus. If that should happen, students
would be removed either by the Fredericton City Police or by a
special contingent of the army from Base Gagetown, twelve miles
from Fredericton. Knight had alerted both these agencies and was
prepared to call them if necessary.

Knowing about these security preparations, I watched the
demonstration of March 20 with some trepidation. The demonstration began at 9:00 am, and according to the *Telegraph-Journal*,
"more than 1,000 UNB students" participated in the protest.
Placard-carrying students paraded around the building and

chanted slogans. Student leaders pledged to fight until their demands were met. Lawson Hunter was greeted with a roar of approval when he told students that if the answers from the board were unsatisfactory, students would have to consider "the possibility of escalation of the protests." Fourth-year arts student Barry Urquhart gave a mock eulogy while a makeshift coffin, representing the Board of Governors and meant to symbolize the "old order" at UNB, was burned in front of the Old Arts Building. "The Board of Governors," Urquhart said, "is for all purposes, quite dead. We bury them because they have not given us what is rightfully ours."[21]

The day passed without incident, although there were some tense moments between the SRC organizers and the radical demonstrators. One of these occurred when one of the radicals, I think it was Dan Weston, grabbed the microphone of the sound truck to urge the demonstrators to occupy the building, only to find that Mike Start had sabotaged his appeal by turning off the power to the amplifier. Another tense moment occurred at the end of the afternoon when the crowds, with encouragement from Weston and John Robinson, started to move into the building. Fortunately, some alert marshals were able to keep the crowds moving and to have them continue out the other side of the building before Brigadier Knight felt he should act.[22]

Colin Mackay, with a delegation from the board, attended a student meeting in the ballroom of the new Student Union Building that evening, where he announced the board's decision. The student reaction was instant and enthusiastic, and Mackay was given a two-minute standing ovation. Mike Start said "the students were jubilant over the board's action."[23] As far as the students were concerned, the affair had been resolved. Weston and the radicals, on the other hand, were "a little pissed off because, you know, Mackay stole our thunder."[24]

Reactions to the board decision were not long in appearing.

Procession following the coffin.

Norman Strax was "extremely happy" that the board had agreed to the arbitration of his case. He felt this was a "victory" for himself and the students. "We have demonstrated that we can defend ourselves. Our next step is to go on and really begin to fight and to kick out those who hold too much power, such as K.C. Irving, and to build a truly democratic society."[25]

J. Laurence Black, a businessman from Sackville, expressed his "grave concern" to Mackay "over the action of your Board in yielding to what appears to be the equivalent of blackmail on the part of the CAUT."[26] On the same day, Ken Cox, the president of NBTel, wrote from Saint John, to observe "that serious problems are seldom solved by appeasement. It is unfortunate that so many professional groups have prostrated their professionalism these days."[27] R. Whidden Ganong of St. Stephen, president of Ganong Brothers, commended Mackay on his "responsible stand in the 'Strax Affair' — that is, up until the developments of the last couple of weeks when it would appear that all your firm resolution is being sabotaged by pressure groups from both the CAUT and the students."[28]

Burning the coffin outside the Board of Governors meeting.

On the day after the board meeting, Mackay reported to Premier Robichaud that he and Education Minister Wendell Meldrum had both agreed "that this was the only course which the board could follow when it was obvious that the University was faced with a very volatile situation."[29] Mackay's personal feelings about the outcome of the dispute were revealed more clearly in a letter he wrote to John Turner the same day. "I don't blame students for a moment," Mackay wrote, "but do feel a great many of them are being conned by CAUT power brokers in Ottawa, aided and abetted by disappointed and disgruntled misfits on faculty. You have no trouble identifying the Marxists on faculty but the difficult ones are those working behind the scene to stab you in the back. Of course, the bulk of the students don't realize this is taking place. Those who do know what is going on are willing to be manipulated for their own student power play. After the Simon Fraser affair[30] I had no illusions about the CAUT method of operation and don't deny the ability of Professor Macpherson, but I do find the actions of the Association to be irresponsible

Student demonstrators, March 20, 1969.

in the extreme."[31] Similarly, in his reply to Murray Sargeant, Mackay wrote, "Of course, we are in the middle of a power play. Unfortunately, the students and most of the faculty don't realize they are being manipulated. The whole thing is a bit like Munich. I can only hope that after this battle the sensible elements will make certain they are to control the University's affairs."[32]

Chapter 10
LIFTING THE CENSURE

March 20 was both the climax and the end of student involvement in the Strax Affair. For most of the students at UNB, the issues connected with the affair had been resolved by the Board of Governors by the end of the month, and life moved on with exams, graduation and summer jobs. For the faculty, however, and the Fredericton and provincial communities, the divisions and suspicions of the affair remained active for at least the next decade.

Once UNB had accepted the terms of the CAUT for the removal of censure on March 20, there remained a tortuous path before it was actually lifted. On March 27, a CAUT delegation of Macpherson, Milner, Smith and Berland met a UNB delegation of Mackay, McAllister, Perry Robinson and university solicitor Bill Hoyt at the Airport Hilton in Montreal. The first step was to agree on the terms for the arbitration and the constitution of the arbitration tribunal, after which UNB agreed to apply to have the injunction lifted.[1] Berland recalled that Mackay accepted the meeting with particularly bad grace, and once the issues were on the table, he "just withdrew. He was lying on the couch looking conspicuously bored by the whole thing and letting us haggle it out."[2]

Door to Old Arts Building

On March 29, Allen Boone wrote to Strax to confirm that his term appointment would finish on June 30, 1969 and would not be renewed.[3] Strax immediately contacted Perry Robinson and argued that there should be nothing in the terms of the arbitration that would prevent the arbitration tribunal from recommending that "Strax be reinstated as a member of the faculty for at least one full year from July 1, 1969." Strax reasoned that, if the arbitration had started in September 1968, it could have recommended his reinstatement for the balance of that academic year.[4]

When negotiations between UNB and the CAUT resumed, the CAUT raised the question of the reinstatement of Strax as a possible outcome of the arbitration. They suggested that he might become a research associate without pay for the 1969–70 academic year but with full access to research facilities and to the use of his NRC research grant. The UNB delegates were adamantly opposed to any reinstatement beyond the current academic year.[5] The revised CAUT draft infuriated Mackay, who felt they had "thrown a curve in the ball park and put us into a new ball game by putting forward the preposterous suggestion that the Arbitration Board be permitted to consider that Professor Strax be kept on past June 30th, 1969. Of course," continued Mackay, "they keep reiterating that this is a matter of simple justice and natural justice and a lot of other God-damned justice. The only kind of justice that Professor Macpherson knows is the kind worked out by J. Stalin in the 1930s."[6]

The CAUT executive would not restrict the arbitration settlement to the 1968–69 academic year and offered UNB the option of either allowing the appointment of Strax to a research position in 1969–70 or, should that not be desirable, of providing Strax with financial compensation not exceeding one year's salary.[7] Mackay put these options to the April 22 meeting of the Board of Governors, which authorized him to empower the arbitration board "to award additional financial compensation to Dr. Strax, in the event of a finding in his favour, in an amount not to exceed one year's salary at the 1968–69 level."[8]

Under those circumstances, the agreement on the terms of the arbitration between UNB and the CAUT was signed off on May 1. The CAUT executive would recommend the lifting of censure to the next meeting of the CAUT Council while, at the

The May 1969 Atlantic Advocate *magazine cover was dedicated to the Strax Affair.*

same time, UNB would apply to dissolve or vacate the injunction against Strax and would defer the issue of costs to the outcome of the arbitration.[9]

UNB's intention to lift the injunction against Strax, however, had not taken Judge Barry into account. The university got on Judge Barry's docket for May 16,[10] when Barry announced that he did not have the authority to dissolve the injunction, since its granting had been a final act by his court which could only be overturned on appeal. He could have varied his original decision if there had been a changed situation or new evidence in the case, but he did not consider the CAUT censure of UNB was such a changed situation, and moreover, he objected to anyone telling the university that it did not have the right to take a matter before the courts. Because it was unusual for a plaintiff to request the removal of an injunction, there was no legal precedent that could be invoked to give Barry jurisdiction in this case. The judge, therefore, dismissed the application on the grounds that he had no legal authority to deal with it, leaving the door open for further applications should either the university or Strax wish to present new evidence.[11]

The university had been represented in Barry's court by Bill Hoyt, and David Nicholson had been an observer for the CAUT. After the hearing, Nicholson reported to Berland that he didn't feel Hoyt had pursued the matter with great vigour in court, explaining that "this may have well been understandable as he was the solicitor who was involved in the original action and therefore it is probably not a reflection of the university's desire to have the injunction lifted, but perhaps only his own personal reluctance in the matter."[12]

Faced with Barry's rejection of the UNB application on the eve of the CAUT Council meeting, Macpherson shot off a telegram to Mackay, telling him that the CAUT executive now considered that UNB, under its agreement with the CAUT, was obliged to appeal Barry's decision to higher courts. The executive would not recommend the lifting of censure unless it received such an assurance before the CAUT Council meeting on May 23.[13] Mackay, on the other hand, felt the agreement between UNB and the CAUT had been concluded in good faith and that the university had taken every step required. In making application, the university had discharged its undertaking, even if the application had not been successful. "An appeal is outside the terms of the agreement," claimed Mackay.[14]

Under these circumstances, the CAUT Council voted on May 23 to sustain the censure on UNB. The council believed that UNB had access to appropriate evidence to lift the injunction on appeal,[15] and Berland quoted Nicholson's report that Hoyt's application to Barry had been half-hearted. The CAUT executive could have recommended lifting censure to the council in the "same lukewarm manner that UNB made the application and be defeated, but it did not want to take that action."[16]

On May 27, Macpherson outlined for Mackay the important changed circumstances that could have been presented to Barry. According to Macpherson, "the university had entered in good faith into arbitration with Professor Strax, and Professor Strax had shown himself willing to adopt orderly procedures for settling his differences with the University. Until the university has vigorously argued the full case for the dissolution of the injunction at either a rehearing or an appeal, the CAUT cannot consider that the University has performed its obligation in respect of the injunction."[17]

At the same time, Willard Allen of the University of Alberta, who replaced Macpherson as president of the CAUT on May 23, forwarded to Mackay — who was also the serving president of the AUCC — the text of another motion inviting the AUCC to join the CAUT in the continuing censure of the president and Board of Governors of the University of New Brunswick.[18] Mackay forwarded the letters from Macpherson and Allen to Bill Hoyt. "Certainly," he quipped, "they sound as if they were bedfellows — perhaps we should attempt to get them to bed down with John

Lennon and Yoko to see if this would enable them to cool the present situation."[19]

The spring of 1969 was also a time to prepare for the selection of the first new president of UNB since 1953. Since no one had been chosen by the June 20 meeting of the Board of Governors, Jim Dineen was appointed acting president for a one-year term following Mackay's scheduled resignation on June 30. But because Mackay would remain president of the AUCC until November 30, the board kept him on as vice-chancellor from July 1 to November 30, even though he would not be president during that time.

The June 20 meeting was Mackay's last as chair. The board decided not to appeal the most recent Barry judgement, but did authorize the president "to institute proceedings for a rehearing on the application made to vacate the injunction, provided that the course will effectively contribute to a resolution of all issues between the university and the CAUT."[20]

Macpherson responded that the CAUT executive would announce the lifting of the censure as soon as a date had been set for a rehearing of the UNB application before Judge Barry.[21] On July 18, Dineen notified Berland, executive secretary of the CAUT, Barry had set August 18 as the date.[22] Berland in turn wired Dineen on the same day that, "in accordance with our agreement the CAUT lifts its censure of the president and board of UNB as of this date."[23]

The arbitration of the Strax case in the summer of 1969 proved even more difficult than some of the other aspects of the affair. As a result of the agreement of May 1, an arbitration tribunal had been set up to consider UNB's treatment of Strax. Earl Palmer, professor of law at the University of Western Ontario, was selected by UNB and the CAUT to act as the reserve chairman of the arbitration board, acting only if the parties to the arbitration failed to agree on a chair.[24] The university chose Arthur Meagher,

The author talks to student Deborah Lyons during the March 1969 demonstration.

professor of law at Dalhousie University, as its representative, and Strax chose Gerry Pacholke, an American who was a lecturer in the mathematics department. Mackay described Pacholke to Meagher in the following terms: "I believe he is bright, but he does view the world and its problems in very simple terms."[25] The two arbitrators agreed to the appointment of Palmer as the chairman of the tribunal.

Palmer scheduled the first meeting of the tribunal for June 12 and 13, but Pacholke responded that these dates were not convenient for Strax or himself. Pacholke noted that "the injunction barring Dr. Strax from the UNB campus was still in effect and might cause delay [because] it prevented Strax from fairly preparing his case." Accordingly, Palmer rescheduled the meeting for July 31 and August 1. On June 30, Pacholke wrote Palmer that the new dates were acceptable to him "provided the injunction has been lifted by July 15." If not, he would not participate in the hearings and would also suggest that Strax not appear. Palmer responded that "it was not a condition of the arbitration that the injunction be lifted. Rather, it was a condition that an honest attempt be made to do so."[26]

Before he left for Fredericton on July 31, Palmer was told that Strax might be unable to attend that morning's hearing, "because of a court action involving his alleged assault on a police officer." Palmer rescheduled the hearing for the afternoon and flew to Fredericton, but neither Strax nor Pacholke showed up for the meeting. Later that day, Pacholke informed Palmer that he was resigning from the tribunal, citing the fact that the injunction against Strax "remains as an instrument of political repression, and encourages further defamation of Dr. Strax's character by slander and/or innuendo." The hearing was no arbitration at all, Pacholke claimed "since it cannot award Strax the position he held prior to his suspension." Pacholke concluded that "while the tribunal has been established to meet the requirements of CAUT policy, I find indefensible and presumptuous the method of choice of chairman for the tribunal followed by the CAUT. That the UNB Board of Governors had the power of veto in the ultimate selection, whereas Dr. Strax was at no time even consulted in this selection, is incredible. If the board was given the right to exclude radicals, hippies or other degenerates from the chairmanship, surely Strax should have been allowed the discretion of excluding university presidents, administrators or whomever else he might find objectionable. The effect of the tribunal will be to becloud the ugly fundamental injustices in the smokescreen of a belated and castrated form of justice: the present hearing."[27]

As Palmer was leaving for the Fredericton airport on August 1, he received a letter from Strax, indicating that he intended to find a new tribunal member to replace Pacholke within seven days and that he still wanted to proceed with the arbitration.[28] Strax wrote again to Palmer on August 7, saying that he had been unable to find anyone and asking that the next meeting of the tribunal be scheduled after August 18, when Barry was scheduled to hear the university's request for a re-hearing on the injunction. Palmer replied that he would wait until he heard further from Strax, since he could not proceed with a two-person arbitration panel.

Hearing nothing from Strax by August 20, Palmer sent a full report on the arbitration to the CAUT, citing Article 16 of the May 1 agreement, which stated that the arbitration tribunal's decision in writing "must be made within three months of its constitution," which would have been on August 13 or, at the latest, August 17. Since that had not happened, Palmer assumed "that this agreement is null and void unless there is 'mutual agreement' between the University and Professor Strax to continue." Palmer felt that UNB had made every effort to assist in the arbitration. "I would be less than candid if I made a similar statement concerning Dr. Strax." As a final comment, Palmer brought out "one aspect of this arbitration which has troubled me greatly," the fact that the CAUT itself had not been a participant in these proceedings. "Quite frankly," he wrote, "I consider that the CAUT has an interest in such arbitration different than that of an individual. Quite obviously, your association (and mine) has an interest in the development of academic due process, a process which should transcend private or regional considerations. In my opinion, such a result is not likely to flow from ad hoc arbitration carried out between large institutions, on one hand, and individuals with various degrees of expertise and interest, on the other. With respect, I suggest that consideration be given in future to having such arbitration carried out with the relevant university on one side, and the CAUT representing the individual involved, as the other party."[29]

On August 21, George McAllister replied to Strax's earlier request for an extension of the arbitration period by telling him the three-month period for arbitration had expired and the university did not intend to extend that period, with the result that the "arbitration provisions of the agreement must be taken as lapsed."[30]

On August 26 Dineen informed Strax that the university had arranged with the CAUT for arbitration to take place and had applied to dissolve or vacate the injunction and that both undertakings had been carried out. The remaining issue was the question of costs and damages, and Dineen now advised Strax "that the university does not intend to enforce, and will not hereafter seek enforcement of, the judgement for damages and costs obtained against you in UNB v. Strax. No other issues remain present to that litigation. In our view, this advice discharges the undertakings made by the university with the Canadian Association of University Teachers."[31]

Judge Barry varied the original injunction against Strax to allow him access to the UNB campus. For the benefit of internal university security, Dineen explained that this meant that Strax had no right to return to the campus and could only be on campus as a visitor subject to UNB granting him permission to visit, a permission that UNB could revoke at any time. At the same time, Strax continued to be restrained "from causing any nuisance or disturbance at the university which would likely have the effect of disrupting the normal operations of the university."[32]

The dispute between UNB and the CAUT was formally brought to an end on September 2 with a letter from Alwyn Berland to Jim Dineen, acknowledging that UNB did not intend to seek enforcement of the judgement for damages and costs obtained against Strax. Berland was disappointed that the academic arbitration had not taken place but recognized that the university had acted in good faith in working toward such arbitration, and that it had obtained a variation on the injunction from Judge Barry. Therefore, "in the view of CAUT, the university has fully discharged its undertakings under the agreement of 1 May 1969."[33]

In October, UNB and the CAUT split the costs of the arbitration.[34] The Strax case was at an end. Colin Mackay wrote to Palmer in early September to thank him for his service with the arbitration tribunal. "It is my hope that the so-called 'Strax Affair' is at an end," wrote Mackay. "It occupied much of the time of many of those associated with the university over a period of nearly 12 months. However, I think it is fair to say that all of us have learned a good deal from the experience and I can only hope that we will be able to profit from it."[35]

Norman Strax's career at the University of New Brunswick ended on July 1, 1969, when his term contract expired and the university stopped his salary. Strax never did have his suspension submitted to arbitration. The allowable period for the arbitration tribunal had expired before the injunction against Strax was lifted. As long as the injunction remained in effect, Strax and his representative on the arbitration panel refused to participate in the arbitration.

Chapter 11
THE ARRIVAL OF THE CORPORATE UNIVERSITY

Unlike many other universities in Canada, student participation in university governance was not really an issue at the University of New Brunswick, since allowance had been made for student representation on the Board of Governors and the Senate in the 1968 *University Act*. Student radicalism at UNB in the latter 1960s initially centred on concern about the continuing war in Vietnam. This concern was promoted by Norman Strax, the young American physics professor, when he sought to energize the radical consciousness of UNB students. When Strax hit upon the introduction of photo-ID cards in September 1968 as symbolic of repression in Canadian society, students were more puzzled than incensed by this purported affront to their rights. As a result, few students participated with him in his rather pathetic demonstrations in the university library.

It was the reaction of President Colin Mackay in suspending Strax, ordering him off the campus and seeking a court injunction to establish that he was indeed a dangerous influence in the university that brought Strax the support he had formerly lacked.

He first secured the support of radical students, who encouraged him to occupy his office and then volunteered to join him in that occupation; he secured the support of a portion of the faculty who had little sympathy for his demonstration but felt that he was being unfairly treated by Mackay; and he secured the support of the radical faculty who reached out to the CAUT and encouraged them to interest themselves in the treatment of Strax. The CAUT, in turn, felt that the treatment of Strax by the UNB administration violated the principles of its Statement on Academic Freedom and Tenure, which UNB had not yet endorsed.

The issue had come to a head during the first year of the implementation of the new *University Act*, which was intended to privilege the teaching faculty by giving it a major voice in the direction of the institution. Yet, the teaching faculty was badly divided by the Strax Affair, as demonstrated by the inability of the AUNBT to formulate any coherent position in response to the situation. This left the door open for the CAUT to take charge, to demand certain actions on the part of the university and ultimately to threaten and then impose public censure on UNB to force the university to adopt its policies.

The CAUT was not immune from criticism in 1969 over its role in the Strax Affair. Having kept quiet for most of the 1968–69 academic year, the Association of Universities and Colleges of Canada (AUCC), the voice of the university presidents, in April 1969, argued that the CAUT Policy Statement on Academic Freedom and Tenure was too narrow in scope, being concerned to protect the freedom of individual members of university teaching staffs from external threats to their academic freedom. However, in recent years, the AUCC statement continued, "we have seen that determined minorities within the university, of either students or staff, can attempt to impose their will on the academic majority and are prepared to use disruptive tactics or even violence to defeat the process of dialogue and persuasion on which academic freedom depends."[1]

S.C. Atkinson, a member of the Board of Governors of the University of Saskatchewan wrote to Mackay that "the whole approach of CAUT to the Strax Affair was not one of conciliation but was a boldfaced attempt at coercion and with the threat of censure I would say that it was very close to attempted blackmail."[2]

The CAUT also received a reprimand from Hugh Saunderson, the president of the University of Manitoba. Saunderson was concerned about the unwillingness of the CAUT to pass any judgement on the behaviour of Strax. "I find this attitude almost incomprehensible. It was this action by Dr. Strax which led up to this entire mess, and yet your Committee said that this was not important and that it hadn't looked into the merits of the matter. Why not? If the CAUT is sincere in its claim to be a professional organization, surely it should be interested in the behaviour of one of its members who had so disrupted the working of the Library that it had to stop providing its normal service. To wash your hands of considering Dr. Strax's prior behaviour, and concentrate all your critical attention on the action of the university in meeting the problem created by Professor Strax seems to me inexcusable in a professional academic body."[3]

***

With the opening of term in September 1969, there was little trace of the student radicalism of the previous year; it appeared as if, for the students, 1968–69 had never happened, and everything seemed to be back to normal. The remaining issues for the SRC concerned the implementation of the 1968 *UNB Act*, with student representation on the Senate and elected students on the Board of Governors. Representation on the Senate was sorted out in 1969, and by 1972 students could be elected to sit as members of the Board of Governors.

A number of the more radical students had moved to Toronto over the summer, some to sample the pleasures of co-operative living in Rochdale College. Before he left office, Mackay was concerned about students "who might give us trouble," such as David Hallam and Nelson Adams, who were in Fredericton and rumoured to be about to set up "a sort of free love community in an old farmhouse in Jemseg" as their version of Rochdale.[4] In early September, Hallam and Clayton Burns sought readmission to their final year of arts and were admitted by the Board of Deans on condition they sign a statement in which they undertook "to obey the regulations of the University without reservations."[5]

Lawson Hunter completed the third year of his law degree in 1969–70. For this degree, Hunter had articled with the firm of McKelvey, Macaulay, Machum and Fairweather in Saint John, where he was under the direction of Neil McKelvey. When Hunter started articling, the lawyers in the firm were wary of letting this radical student near their important files and assigned another lawyer to keep an eye on him. By the time Hunter graduated in 1970, however, McKelvey told him that he was the best articling student they had ever had. At the same time, McKelvey warned him that, because of his radical activities at UNB, including his support of Strax and Tom Murphy, there were rumours that members of the New Brunswick Bar, including Judge Barry himself, were going to object to his admission to the bar. While Hunter knew that he had the support of McKelvey and of Bill Ryan, the dean of law, he decided not to apply right away for bar admission, but to let things cool down a bit in New Brunswick. Accordingly, he went to Harvard in 1970 to take a master's degree in law, returning to New Brunswick in the following year when he was admitted to the bar with no opposition.

Hunter moved to Ottawa in the 1970s to work for the federal government. Although Mackay was also working there, their paths rarely crossed, and when they did Mackay went to the other side of the street to avoid him. Gordon Fairweather, also in Ottawa as the member of Parliament for Fundy-Royal, felt this continuing feud between Hunter and Mackay was silly, so he brought them together at a reception at the National Art Centre, in a plot cooked up with Mary Louise Lynch, a Saint John lawyer and a good friend of both Fairweather and Mackay. The preparations for the encounter were such that, when Hunter approached Mackay at the National Art Centre reception, the conversation was easy and their reconciliation was launched.[6]

Tom Murphy spent the 1969–70 academic year in Toronto as the national president of the Student Christian Movement. Because of its involvement with radical social issues and its lesser concern with prayer and devotion in the late 1960s, the SCM lost support from a number of its church sponsors, who reduced their funding for the organization, both at the national level and also at UNB. The decline in support from the local churches for UNB meant that the SCM Advisory Council had to release George Mossman as its general secretary at the end of June 1969.[7] During his period as national president, Murphy very much encouraged involvement in issues of social justice. One example of this involvement was the SCM-sponsored travelling seminar for students in the Atlantic provinces in late May 1970, which underlined the role of the SCM as a radical voice in national debates.[8]

Tom Murphy returned to Fredericton in the 1970s, where he opened a health-food store, "Harmony Earth," and later a healthy restaurant, "The Attic." In the early 1980s he completed his BA and an MA in Sociology at UNB, after which he enrolled in a doctoral program at Cornell.[9]

***

The appointment of Jim Dineen as acting president in the summer of 1969 brought a breath of fresh air to the administration of

UNB. A conservative traditionalist who had been the most loyal and vocal supporter of Mackay through the crises of the previous year, Dineen was essentially a pragmatist who realized that issues left over from the previous year had to be dealt with in an open and timely fashion. "If you sweep a problem under the rug," he is quoted as saying, "you will always get a bump."[10] Above all, he realized he had inherited a wounded institution in need of healing, a task for which he had both the personality and the skills.

His appointment led to a new openness on campus, and also to attention being paid to issues that demanded attention. At its meeting on September 3, 1969, the Board of Deans decided, in the interests of transparency, that the minutes of its meetings should, for the first time, be circulated.[11] A new monthly publication was introduced on September 17, the *University Gazette*, designed to inform board members, faculty, staff and students about official academic and administrative policy decisions and other university business. Appropriately, its first issue published documents relating to the Strax Affair from the summer months, including a full transcript of the hearing before Judge Barry to vary the injunction against Strax.[12] In the spirit of the 1968 *UNB Act*, the faculty deans of the 1970s sought to encourage and promote faculty involvement in the governance of their faculties.[13]

One of the areas in need of review was campus security policy. In the fall of 1969, the role of the Security Section was more clearly defined and it was given more professional leadership. Its role would be limited to performing "watch keeping and traffic control assignments," while the University would make use of the Fredericton City Police and the RCMP "for assistance in investigation of offences and due process of the law." By early October a draft policy on "University Security Organization" was ready for submission to the Board of Governors.[14]

On November 26 Dineen convened his first meeting of the university committee to discuss terms and conditions of employment

James Dineen, President and Vice-Chancellor of UNB, May 1972.

and the applicability of the CAUT Policy on Academic Freedom and Tenure at UNB. As with the Board of Deans, the minutes of this committee were to be distributed extensively and in a more timely way than previously.[15]

In late 1969 Dineen was appointed to the presidency in his own right, with a term running from January 1, 1970 to June 30, 1976. The appointment was supported enthusiastically by the university community, who now trusted his instincts and his capacity for restoring cohesion to the university. It was an institutional tragedy for UNB when Dineen contracted terminal cancer and had to resign the presidency in June 1972. He died in September, 1975. Steve Patterson felt that Dineen was a different kind of person from Mackay. "There was certainly nothing leftish in his approach, but he did recognize that participation was important." He ran an open administration and "proved in a relatively short period of time that you could have both level-headedness and moderation. In his very short presidency, he gave us a lot."[16] Israel Unger, when he was president of the AUNBT, had worked with Dineen and believed he "was a man of substance, a genuinely warm person and very, very interested in unifying the institution and doing the right thing. Within a year he had taken the heat out of the university."[17]

In 1971 Colin Mackay took on a new position as executive director of the AUCC, a job he held for four years. Les Shemilt noted that his work with the AUCC was less than a success since Mackay's personality and approach were not really amenable to working in a supportive role with university presidents.[18] In the late 1970s he served on several Canadian delegations to the United Nations and also worked as an adviser to the Canadian International Development Agency (CIDA). He was especially successful in encouraging the development of university education in Botswana, Lesotho, Swaziland and Kenya and visited Africa many times during the rest of his life.

As a result of the conflicts surrounding the Strax Affair and the sense that UNB was heading in a new direction after his departure, Mackay's connection with UNB had been rather anomalous since his resignation. With his reputation under a cloud, it had been difficult to determine what role he should play at the university. This situation was rectified somewhat in 1978 when he was named the first president emeritus of the university, and in 1979 when the lawn between the men's residences and the Student Union Building was designated the Mackay Promenade. When Jim Downey[19] became UNB President in 1980, he deliberately brought Mackay back into public prominence. As president emeritus, Mackay was frequently used by Downey during convocation and Encaenia ceremonies to introduce and look after some of the special guests. He was provided with his own office on the Saint John campus and remained an active presence at the university until his death in 2003 at the age of 83.

***

Colin B. Mackay had the vision, the imagination, the energy and the connections to build the University of New Brunswick as a modern comprehensive research university with a national and international reputation. Not only did he find the bricks and mortar and the faculty to house and teach the ever-increasing student body, but he also steered the university toward a new and more democratic constitution in the design of the *University of New Brunswick Act* of 1968. Before 1968 UNB had been a presidential autocracy. Under Mackay's dynamic leadership, initiative rested primarily in the hands of the president, supported by the faculty deans and other senior administrators. This presidential "cabinet" made up a majority of the membership of the internal University Council, which also included some faculty representatives. The president reported to a Senate, made up of members outside the university who were named by the provincial government and by the alumni. Since the president chaired both bodies, they served primarily as sounding boards for his initiatives.

With the 1968 *UNB Act*, a radical change was introduced in the governance of the university. The intent of the Duff-Berdahl Report and of UNB's University Committee was that a new era of collegial governance should be inaugurated, with power vested in the teaching faculty and modelled on the ideal of the community of scholars. Under the new act, the University Council would be renamed the Senate, would be responsible for all academic affairs of the university and would always have a majority of members who belonged to the teaching faculty. The academic administrators would constitute a minority, giving the teaching faculty the dominant voice in internal academic matters. The former Senate was to be renamed the Board of Governors, and while it would continue to have a majority of external appointees from the government and the alumni, it would also have four representatives of the teaching faculty. Where the Board of Governors would be responsible for financial and non-academic matters, this would also mean that the teaching faculty could have a significant voice in deliberations on matters of finance and personnel policy.

Colin Mackay had built the modern UNB, and by 1968 he had agreed that the running of the university should be placed in the hands of the teaching faculty. Mackay himself recognized the change in the institution and submitted his resignation as president in December 1968, citing the reason that he was not a democrat and that a new university had been created, which should be governed by others.

The Strax Affair, however, negated many of these democratic aspirations. President Mackay, in securing an injunction against Strax, was unprepared to allow the Board of Governors, and particularly the faculty governors, to try to resolve the crisis of the institution. At the same time, the teaching faculty proved incapable of setting aside its differences and its suspicions, to make decisions for the greater good of the institution. Because of this, the university administrators, wary of faculty radicalism, held the administration to be the true guardians of the well-being of the institution. The result was that during the 1970s, the administration came to exercise greater power at UNB without the faculty playing the legislative and mediating role that had been intended for it by the 1968 *UNB Act*. The students, who had not been paid more than token attention in the act, became an active voice during the Strax Affair and became another interest to be reckoned with in the university. Rather than being a community of scholars, the university showed that it was really a collection of corporate interests: those of the faculty, the students and the administration. The intervention of the CAUT supported the interests of the faculty where terms and conditions of their employment were concerned, and in supporting Strax, directly challenged the interests of the administration. Rather than the university being governed by the collegial ideal of the community of scholars, within a year of the new *UNB Act*, issues in the university came to be resolved through a power struggle between the corporate interests, as the dominant interest of the administrative clique was challenged by the active voices of the faculty and the students.

The resolution of the conflict between Mackay and the CAUT in March 1969 left UNB in an institutional shambles, with only the good sense and pragmatism of Jim Dineen to try to restore some internal confidence and cohesion. The only institution that benefited from the Strax Affair was the CAUT, which used the events at UNB to enhance its national prominence and national influence.[20] The prospects of collegiality at UNB in 1969 were remote at best in an institution with such a high level of distrust and lack of empathy between the "radicals" and the "dinosaurs."

In 1968, there had been a lot of sympathy among the faculty for the building of a collegial university. On the one hand, the collegial nature of the AUNBT membership, which included academic administrators along with members of the teaching faculty, was one aspect of this, as was the strongly expressed view of many that the AUNBT should remain a professional asso-ciation and never become a trade union. On the other hand, the CAUT looked at universities in terms of the labour-management relationship between university governors and administration, faculty and staff, and thought primarily of the corporate uni-versity as the model. While many in the CAUT sought faculty unionization, they also realized it was not politically acceptable in the universities of the late 1960s and early 1970s when, if UNB is any example, many faculty members believed that unionization would interfere with its collegial community.

Chemist Israel Unger was elected to succeed Perry Robinson as president of the AUNBT in April 1969. Because the membership was so badly divided, Unger saw that his first task was to heal the wounds in his organization.[21] He felt that whatever information the AUNBT executive had on the Strax Affair should be circulated to the membership, since "members of the university faculty should not act precipitously without knowing all the facts."[22]

In spite of these initiatives by the AUNBT executive, faculty divisions persisted between those who supported the actions of the CAUT and those who did not. On December 4, 1969 Unger received a letter signed by nine faculty members registering "the concern of approximately 80 per cent of the members of the Faculties of Education, Engineering, Forestry, Law and Nursing about the current philosophy and practices of the AUNBT." The authors felt that the approach of the AUNBT "is primarily based on trade union practices rather than those appropriate for a professional association," and concluded "that the AUNBT does not represent the views of a large number of faculty members of this university."[23] The validity of the complaint was confirmed when it was noticed that all current members of the AUNBT executive came from either arts or science.[24] The executive realized that a split in the AUNBT, which would lead to the professional faculties creating their own organization, would weaken the position of the faculty in the university and was to be avoided at all costs.[25]

During the 1970s the AUNBT and the administration worked through the University Committee to develop a faculty manual by negotiating terms and conditions of employment and by instituting a grievance arbitration provision. This was an important initiative by the Dineen administration to address personnel policy in a collegial fashion. Attitudes toward unionization were to change at UNB in the 1970s, because of the economic slowdown resulting from the oil crisis and the rampant inflation of that decade. From the mid-1970s the CAUT began a serious push for faculty unionization across Canada.

The situation at UNB in the late 1970s was also marked by a lack of faculty confidence in John Anderson, who had succeeded Dineen as president in 1973. Anderson had joined the biology department at UNB in 1958, but in 1967 had left to become the director of the Fisheries Research Station in St. Andrews, New Brunswick. Because he had not participated in the events of 1968–69 at UNB, he had neither a feel for the culture of the community, nor a sense of how the university needed to be handled following the Strax Affair. This was demonstrated when he launched a strategic planning exercise and created great fear among the faculty that declining resources would be dealt with by the reduction of the teaching faculty.[26] It was also demonstrated when his administration refused to extend the collegial discussions of the University Committee to include any faculty involvement in the determination of faculty salaries.[27]

Although there had been extensive opposition to the idea of the AUNBT as a trade union in the late 1960s, by the end of the 1970s many faculty, including myself, believed that unionization was the only way our rights and our level of income could be protected. The AUNBT declared itself a trade union in 1977 and at the beginning of 1978 applied to the New Brunswick Industrial Relations Board for certification as the bargaining agent for full-time academics. Certification was achieved in 1979, and the first collective agreement between the AUNBT and the Board of Governors was concluded on November 3, 1980.[28]

In spite of the fact that the Strax Affair interfered with the establishment of a collegial campus in Fredericton, the opening of a second campus in Saint John in 1964 added a structural impediment to collegiality in the university as a whole. The campus was opened in recognition that a significant portion of the population of Saint John and southern New Brunswick could not afford to leave home for a university education and also in response to political pressure from the Saint John business community, which believed that the largest city in New Brunswick deserved to have its own university. The creation of the second campus was opposed by many faculty on the Fredericton campus from the beginning. They viewed it as a response to parochial politics that threatened to disperse the limited resources available to the Fredericton campus with its active and ambitious research and graduate programs. Under the 1968 *UNB Act*, the university Senate was made up of faculty from both campuses, the majority of whom were from Fredericton.

Initially started as a two-year feeder school for the Fredericton campus, the Saint John campus suffered from the lack of enthusiasm of the Fredericton faculty and also from the failure of the university administration, forced to work in this tangle of New Brunswick politics, to define an academic rationale for the existence of a two-campus university. By the 1970s the Saint John campus wanted to expand its program to become a full-year degree-granting branch of UNB. While this was approved by the university Senate, these major changes in the position of the Saint John campus had to be supported by calling on existing favours and the goodwill between the campuses.[29] In the early 1980s, in his first term as president, Jim Downey struck a special Committee to Review Inter-Campus Relations (CRICR), which recommended that the university Senate should be eliminated in favour of one Senate for each campus. The debate in the Senate on its abolition was fierce and the vote was close. Downey himself vacated the chair at one point to speak in favour of the adoption of the report and the associated abolition of one university Senate.

Two senates meant that it would be difficult, if not impossible, for the teaching faculty to make collegial decisions for the whole university. With unionization, the relationship between management and labour would be determined by the countervailing powers inherent in the collective bargaining system. Even the students adapted to the model when the SRC was replaced on the Fredericton campus by the Student Union. Between the 1970s and the 1990s the ideal of the collegial university gave way at UNB to the reality and the mentality of the corporate university, where the university was modelled on a business corporation, with a board of directors, chief executive officer and executive group, an expensive faculty workforce and a host of student clients and customers. The collegial university had become the corporate university, as it has remained at UNB to the present day.

✳✳✳

Norman Strax remained in Fredericton for another ten years and continued his struggle with the forces of repression. Strax had never been really interested in issues of faculty rights within the university apart from those that bore directly on his own situation. The debates of the CAUT and the AUNBT had left him cold and his lack of respect for institutional due process was demonstrated when he refused to co-operate with the arbitration board appointed to hear his case. Strax operated from a completely different perspective on the question of rights. His view was that rights were inherent in free individuals and that any institutional structure only imposed illegitimate limitations on the free exercise of these rights. The task, as he saw it, was to remove institutional restrictions on individual freedoms wherever possible and to show how individuals were being stifled and suffocated by the administration of complex institutions, such as the university. Institutional authority, by definition, could never be exercised benevolently.[30]

Strax continued to live in his cabin on the Royal Road, on the northern outskirts of Fredericton. Radicals and former radicals kept in touch with him and were concerned about his health and well-being. For transportation he had his Volkswagen beetle in which, Dan Weston recalls, the floor was always rusted out and he only had one seat. He was often flat broke, could not pay his rent and lived for a long time "on flour and macaroni and whatever

Lawson Hunter delivering a graduation address after he had been awarded an honorary Doctor of Laws by UNB in 2011.

money he could scrape up that people gave to him."[31]

I last saw Norman Strax in the fall of 1979. During the 1978–79 academic year, Tom Murphy and I had organized a study group on the Strax Affair for discussion and reflection on the events of ten years earlier. We had held several meetings throughout the year and had deliberately invited neither Colin Mackay nor Norman Strax to attend, wanting a relatively dispassionate discussion of the event. History graduate student Marc Milner had been assigned to work with us in compiling a small archive of documents and correspondence relating to the affair.

The seminar had been so successful that, in the fall of 1979, we decided to continue it and to invite Strax to tell us how he saw the affair after ten years. We met him in a room in the Student Union Building, but nothing went as planned. To start with, Strax was annoyed that we had been discussing "his" affair for a year without inviting him. When he was asked to offer his perspective on the affair, he refused to do so, saying that the real issue to be discussed was why Peter Kent had continued to support and to work for such an arbitrary and destructive regime as that headed by Colin Mackay. As I recall it, Tom Murphy did his best to mediate the discussion that ensued for the remainder of the meeting. At the end of the meeting, Strax asked if he could borrow our boxed archives on the Strax Affair. Since we were operating a free enquiry on the affair we agreed, Strax took the archives, and that was the last any of us saw of them. Murphy tried to get them back, but Strax refused to part with them and we could only assume they had been destroyed.

Shortly after that, Strax got a job at Wabash College, a liberal arts college for men in Crawfordsville, Indiana and left Fredericton. In 1991 he was diagnosed with prostate cancer and became disabled. After that, he and his wife Jacqueline devoted their lives to raising money for prostate cancer research. In 1999 an e-mail from his wife indicated they were then living in New York State. In 2002 he succumbed to the cancer.

His obituary in the *Princeton Alumni Weekly* told his life history up until his teaching career at UNB, but became rather vague on specifics after that. I felt this was a tragic conclusion to an important life experience that needed to be captured for posterity. Norman Strax had the potential to become a brilliant physicist but had devoted his life and sacrificed his academic career to opposing the injustice of institutional oppression, whether it was directed against the people of Vietnam, against student protestors or against the students and people of New Brunswick. In doing so, his idealism inspired a great number of young people whose lives were marked by association with his determination to change the world for the better. For that, he deserves to be remembered.

ENDNOTES

CHAPTER 1

1 Broadsheet "Fuck the ID Cards." UNB Archives.

2 Interview with David Cox, August 24, 2000.

3 Note by Mackay from discussion with Brig. Knight, September 26, 1968. UNB Archives, Presidential Papers, Series 9, Sub-series 2, Box 69, File 100.

4 Bailey to all members of faculty, August 9, 1968. UNB Archives, Presidential Papers, Series 9, Sub-series 2, Box 69, File 100.

5 Interview with Lawson Hunter, August 7, 2000.

6 Broadsheet: "Play Bookie-book Today!" and "Why we should chuck the ID Cards." UNB Archives and interview with Tom Murphy, August 26, 2000.

7 Gunn to Mackay, "Anti-ID Card Protesters at Library," September 25, 1968. UNB Archives, Presidential Papers, Series 9, Sub-series 2, Box 69, File 100.

8 Minutes of the Board of Governors, September 28, 1968, UNB Archives.

9 Mackay to Strax, September 24, 1968. UNB Archives, Presidential Papers, Series 9, Sub-series 2, Box 69, File 100.

10 Interview with Tom Murphy, August 26, 2000; Interview with Dan Weston, August 23, 2002. Tom Murray supports the contention that the occupation was Tom Murphy's idea in "Some Remembrances and Thoughts on my Participation in the Strax Affair, Fredericton, New Brunswick, 1968." While Murphy and Weston disagree on the genesis of the plan to occupy the office, they both agree that the idea did not originate with Strax.

11 Hugo Johnston, *Radical Campus: Making Simon Fraser University.* Vancouver and Toronto: Douglas and McIntyre, 2005.

12 Tim and Julyan Reid (eds.), *Student Power and the Canadian Campus.* Toronto: Peter Martin Associates, Ltd., 1969.

13 Dorothy Eber, *The Computer Centre Party: Canada Meets Black Power.* Montreal: Tundra Books, 1969.

14 Duart Farquharson, *Confrontation on the Campus.* Ottawa: Southam News Service, January 1969; Roberta Lexier, "The Community of Scholars: The English-Canadian Student Movement and University Governance," in Marie Hammond-Callaghan and Matthew Hayday (eds.), *Mobilizations, Protests and Engagements: Canadian Perspectives on Social Movements.* Halifax and Winnipeg: Fernwood Publishing, 2008; P.B. Waite, *The Lives of Dalhousie University, Volume Two: 1925–1980.* Montreal and Kingston: McGill-Queen's University Press, 1998.

CHAPTER 2

1 Interview with R.G.L. Fairweather, August 15, 2002.

2 Ibid.

3 Ibid.

4 Interview with Les Shemilt, August 26, 2000.

5 Susan Montague, *A Pictorial History of the University of New Brunswick*. Fredericton: UNB, 1992, p. 141.

6 R.A. Tweedie, *On With The Dance: A New Brunswick Memoir 1935–1960*, Saint John: New Ireland Press, 1986, pp. 161–65.

7 Interview with R.G.L. Fairweather, August 15, 2002.

8 Ibid.

9 Ibid.

10 Ibid.

11 Interview with Les Shemilt, August 26, 2000; Basanta Kumar Mahato graduated with his doctorate at Encaenia in May 1967.

12 Interviews with Stephen Patterson (August 17, 2000), David Cox (August 24, 2000), Alwyn Berland (August 26, 2000), Dan Weston (August 23, 2002), John Oliver (August 2, 2002) and Murray Young (June 7, 2002).

13 Doug Owram, *Born at the Right Time: A History of the Baby-Boom Generation*. Toronto: University of Toronto Press, 1996.

14 John G. Reid, "Some Historical Reflections on the Report of the Royal Commission on Higher Education in New Brunswick, 1962." Unpublished manuscript, 1989.

15 By 1969, only 19 per cent of the students were enrolled in engineering, and if this was added to students enrolled in the Faculties of Science and Forestry it only accounted for 35 per cent of the student body as compared to 70 per cent for the same faculties in 1953. It was the Faculty of Arts that had sustained the greatest growth over the previous decade. In 1969, 28 per cent of the students were enrolled in arts, and if that figure was added to what might be called the "applied arts" — programs of law, education and business administration — it accounted for 51 per cent of the student body.

This continuing growth of the university was very much a feature of the Mackay years at UNB. In the 1950s, there were annual increases in the student population of 13 per cent and, in the 1960s, of 12 per cent. Only in 1972 did the university experience a decline in its population growth rate, and throughout the 1970s the university population levelled off with an average annual growth rate of 1.8 per cent.

16 The UNB Calendars between 1953 and 1969 include detailed population statistics for the university, and therefore provide an excellent source for assessing the changing size and composition of the university. In 1968–69, 4,792 students — more than five times the population of 1953 — were being taught by 318 faculty members, about five times the faculty complement of 1953.

17 Draft of *Atlantic Advocate* article, April 23, 1968. UNB Archives, Presidential Papers, Series 10, Sub-series 1, Box 86, File 331.

18 David M . Cameron, *More Than an Academic Question: Universities, Government, and Public Policy in Canada*. Halifax: The Institute for Research on Public Policy, 1991, pp. 124–25.

19 Currently the University of Winnipeg.

20 Michiel Horn, *Academic Freedom in Canada: A History*. Toronto: University of Toronto Press, 1999; Kenneth McNaught, *Conscience and History: A Memoir*. Toronto: University of Toronto Press, 1999; Peter C. Kent, "The Unrealized Potential of Canada's Universities," *Acadiensis*, Vol. 31, no, 2 (Spring 2002); Interview with Les Shemilt, August 26, 2000.

21 Cameron, *More Than an Academic Question*, p. 321.

22 These issues are also discussed in Horn, *Academic Freedom*, especially Chapters 11 and 12.

23 Cameron, *More Than an Academic Question*, Chapter 7.

24 Johnston, *Radical Campus*; Lexier, "The Community of Scholars."

25 Minutes of the University Committee (No. 6), May 4, 1967. UNB Archives, Bailey Papers, case 82, File 3.

26 Minutes of the University Committee (No. 3), March 30, 1967; (No. 5), April 25, 1967; (No. 6), May 4, 1967; and Notes by Bailey on the Meeting of March 30. UNB Archives, Bailey Papers, case 82, File 3.

CHAPTER 3

1 Cyril Levitt, *Children of Privilege: Student Revolt in the Sixties, A Study of Student Movements in Canada, the United States and West Germany*. Toronto: University of Toronto Press, 1984.

2 For the impact of the creation of the Université de Moncton, see Donald J. Savoie, *I'm from Bouctouche, Me*. Montreal and Kingston: McGill-Queen's University Press, 2009.

3 Della M.M. Stanley, *Louis Robichaud; A Decade of Power*. Halifax: Nimbus Publishing Limited, 1984; Michel Cormier, *Louis J. Robichaud: A Not So Quiet Revolution*. Translated by Jonathan Kaplansky. Moncton: Faye Editions, 2004; E.R. Forbes and D.A. Muise (eds.), *The Atlantic Provinces in Confederation*. Toronto: University of Toronto Press and Fredericton: Acadiensis Press, 1993; Pasolli, Lisa, "Bureaucratizing the Atlantic Revolution: The 'Saskatchewan Mafia' in the New Brunswick Civil Service, 1960–1970." *Acadiensis* Vol. 38, no. 1 (Winter/Spring 2009), 126-50.

4 For a broader discussion, see Bryan D. Palmer, *Canada's 1960s: The Ironies of Identity in a Rebellious Era*. Toronto: University of Toronto Press, 2009.

5 Pierre Berton, *1967: The Last Good Year*. Toronto: Doubleday Canada Limited, 1997.

6 Reid, *Student Power*.

7 Lexier, "The Community of Scholars." p. 126; see also Cyril Levitt, *Children of Privilege: Student Revolt in the Sixties, A Study of Student Movements in Canada, the United States and West Germany*. Toronto: University of Toronto Press, 1984; Reid and Reid, *Student Power*; Farquharson, *Confrontation on the Campus*; Dorothy Eber, *The Computer Centre Party: Canada Meets Black Power*. Montreal: Tundra Books, 1969.

8 Johnston, *Radical Campus*.

9 Kenneth Strand, the new president, immediately adopted the CAUT policy for academic freedom and tenure and reduced the size of the Board of Governors. As a result of these changes, censure was lifted in November 1968.

The Politics, Sociology and Anthropology Department at Simon Fraser was placed under trusteeship in 1968 in an attempt to secure a committee on promotion and tenure that did not include students. The result was a strike by the department in which its services were withdrawn from the university. The administration thereupon suspended eight members of the PSA Department and incurred another CAUT censure in 1971.

10 These residences still exist as McLeod House and Magee House in the UNB residence program.

11 Interview with Lawson Hunter, August 7, 2000.

12 Interview with Tom Murphy, August 26, 2000.

13 Interview with Stephen Patterson, August 17, 2000.

14 Interview with Les Shemilt, August 26, 2000.

15 On the SCM, see Robin Boyd, *The Witness of the Student Christian Movement. Church ahead of the Church.* London: SPCK, 2007; Catherine Gidney, "Poisoning the Student Mind?: The Student Christian Movement at the University of Toronto, 1920–1965." *Journal of the Canadian Historical Association, 1997,* New Series, Vol. 8.

16 Interview with Les Shemilt, August 26, 2000.

17 "Values, Change, and Action — 67" brochure, UNB Archives, Presidential Papers, Series 9, Sub-series 2, Box 73, File 249.

18 David Mendell, *Obama: From Promise to Power.* New York: Amistad, 2007, p. 67.

19 Interview with John Oliver, August 2, 2002.

20 Interview with Tom Murphy, August 26, 2000.

21 Interview with Lawson Hunter, August 7, 2000.

22 Interview with Tom Murphy, August 26, 2000.

23 Interview with John Oliver, August 2, 2002.

24 Interview with David Jonah, August 15, 2000.

25 Interview with David Cox, August 24, 2000.

26 The story was told by Strax to Alwyn Berland. Interview with Alwyn Berland, August 26, 2000.

27 Obituary of Norman Strax in 2002, Princeton Alumni Web Page, http://www.princeton.edu/paw/memorials/memorials_1950s/memorials_1957.html; obituary of Philip Strax, *New York Times,* March 11, 1999.

28 Boone to Mackay, November 23, 1966. UNB Archives, C.W. Argue Papers, Series 1, Sub-series 2, Box 4, File 66.

29 Interview with Tom Murphy, August 26, 2000; Interview with John Oliver, August 2, 2002.

30 Interview with Tom Murphy, August 26, 2000; interview with Dan Weston, August 23, 2002.

31 E-mail from Franz Martin to the author, April 17, 2010.

32 Interviews with Alwyn Berland (August 26, 2000), John Earl (June 20, 2002), Lawson Hunter (August 7, 2000), David Jonah (August 15, 2000), Tom Murphy (August 26, 2000), John Oliver (August 2, 2002), Stephen Patterson (August 17, 2000), and Dan Weston (August 23, 2002).

33 Terry H. Anderson, *The Movement and the Sixties: Protest in America from Greensboro to Wounded Knee.* New York: Oxford University Press, 1995, pp. 177–80.

34 Circular letter from Strax to colleagues, October 13, 1967. UNB Archives, Barry Toole Papers.

35 Smith to Mackay, October 30, 1967. UNB Archives, Presidential Papers, Series 9, Sub-series 2, Box 75, File 297.

36 Churchill to Mackay, October 25, 1967. UNB Archives, Presidential Papers, Series 9, Sub-series 2, Box 75, File 297.

37 Cann to Board of Governors, October 26, 1967. UNB Archives, Presidential Papers, Series 9, Sub-series 2, Box 75, File 297.

38 "Investigate Now" (editorial). *King's County Record,* October 26, 1967.

39 "A worried Mother and Dad to Mackay," November 14, 1967, UNB Archives, Presidential Papers, Series 9, Sub-series 2, Box 75, File 297.

40 Cox was elected on February 11, 1968, inheriting plans for the protest march that had been

developed under his predecessor, Wayne Beach. Tom Murphy chaired the March Coordinating Committee. SRC Minutes for February 18, 1968, UNB Archives.

41 Interview with David Cox, August 24, 2000.

42 Interview with Tom Murphy, August 26, 2000.

43 Interview with David Cox, August 24, 2000.

44 "They're Peeping, Not Looking." *Kings County Record*, February 29, 1968.

45 Mackay to Robichaud, February 23, 1968. UNB Archives, Presidential Papers, Series 9, Sub-series 2, Box 67, File 48; Mackay to Meldrum, February 23, 1968. UNB Archives, Presidential Papers, Series 9, Sub-series 2, Box 67, File 49.

46 Hal Winter, "The strange case of doctor Norman Strax or how 'protesting' was started at old UNB." *The Gazette*, Montreal, November 9, 1968.

47 Boone to Strax, April 22, 1968. UNB Archives, Presidential Papers, Series 9, Sub-series 2, Box 69, File 100.

48 Sears to Mackay, July 2, 1968. UNB Archives, C.W. Argue Papers, Series 1, Sub-series 2, Box 4, File 66.

49 Boone to Strax, May 31, 1968. UNB Archives, Presidential Papers, Series 9, Sub-series 2, Box 69, File 100.

50 Boone to Strax, July 31, 1968. UNB Archives, Presidential Papers, Series 9, Sub-series 2, Box 69, File 100.

51 Strax to Boone, August 5, 1968. UNB Archives, Presidential Papers, Series 9, Sub-series 2, Box 69, File 100.

52 Interview with Lawson Hunter, August 7, 2000.

53 Interview with Stephen Patterson, August 17, 2000.

54 Interview with Lawson Hunter, August 7, 2000.

CHAPTER 4

1 Senate Minutes, February 15, May 15 and June 19, 1968. UNB Archives.

2 Interviews with Les Shemilt, August 26, 2000; and Murray Young, June 7, 2002.

3 Interview with John Earl, June 20, 2002.

4 Interview with Harold Sharp, August 14, 2000.

5 Final Report, "Committee on the Circumstances of the Suspension of Dr. Norman Strax," November 1, 1968. UNB Presidential Papers/ S9/ SS2/ 69/ F103.

6 Monohan to members of the CAUT executive and Finance Committee, October 11, 1968. National Archives of Canada, MG 28/ Series 1208/ Vol. 17/ 300 Academic Freedom and Tenure (Strax Case), QU-25859.

7 Interview with Les Shemilt, August 26, 2000.

8 Interview with Marion Rogers (Mrs. Howard Rogers), November 20, 1993.

9 UNB Board of Governors, Minutes of the Meeting of October 8, 1968. UNB Archives.

CHAPTER 5

1 Interview with Tom Murphy, August 26, 2000.

2 Ibid.

3 Franz Martin, unpublished journal, September 8–October 6, 1968.

4 Interview with Stephen Patterson, August 17, 2000.

5 Martin journal, October 7–8, 1968.

6 Interview with John Oliver, August 2, 2002.

7 Interview with Les Shemilt, August 26, 2000.

8 Thomas A. Murray, "Some Remembrances and Thoughts On My Participation in the *Strax Affair*, Fredericton, New Brunswick, 1968." Unpublished manuscript.

9 Interview with Dan Weston, August 23, 2002.

10 Martin journal, October 10–26, 1968.

11 Interview with Lawson Hunter, August 7, 2000.

12 Martin journal, October 28–November 11, 1968.

13 Interview with Murray Young, June 7, 2002.

14 Interview with John Earl, June 20, 2002.

15 Interview with Stephen Patterson, August 17, 2000.

CHAPTER 6

1 Interview with David Cox, August 24, 2000.

2 Martin journal, November 13–17, 1968.

3 SRC Minutes, November 17, 1968. UNB Archives.

4 Interview with Lawson Hunter, August 7, 2000.

5 Blue to Green, November 20, 1968. UNB Archives, Bailey Papers, 80/ F22.

6 Martin journal, November 17–20, 1968.

7 Minutes of a Special Meeting of the SRC, November 20, 1968. UNB Archives.

8 Minutes of the CAUT Council, November 16–17, 1968, and CAUT Council Meeting resumé prepared by Doug Brewer. UNB Archives, H.A. Sharp papers, Series 3, Box 5, F5.

9 Interview with Murray Young, June 7, 2002.

10 Interview with Harold Sharp, August 14, 2000.

11 Sharp to Smith, December 11, 1968. UNB Archives, AUNBT Records, Box 7/ F1.

12 Sharp to Smith, February 13, 2008. UNB Archives, Sharp Papers, Series 3, Box 5, F5.

13 Pacey to Macpherson, November 19, 1968. UNB Archives, Bailey Papers, 80/ F22.

14 The AUNBT deplores the delay by the University Administration in establishing prompt and just procedures, consistent with those outlined by the AUNBT and the CAUT, for investigation and adjudication of the charges of misconduct made against Professor Norman Strax, and insists that such procedures be at once established.

The AUNBT regards the precipitous and continuing resort to legal proceedings as an abdication by the university of its proper authority, and condemns that abdication of authority as unworthy of the principles to which the university is dedicated.

At the same time, however, the AUNBT equally deplores any deliberate obstruction by individuals of the proper business of the university, namely education and research, especially when dictated by a deliberate refusal to employ the established channels of University and Student Government.

Therefore, the AUNBT calls on the University Administration to do all in its power to return any outstanding cases of possible student or faculty misconduct to within the framework of the university's various governing bodies, including the faculty association and the student government, where they rightly belong, and calls on the University Administration to institute proper university adjudication of these cases.

If this action is not carried out, the AUNBT should find out promptly which exact branches of the University Administration are directly responsible for its not being carried out, and should vote non-confidence in those branches.

15 Minutes of the AUNBT General Meeting, November 26, 1968. UNB Archives, AUNBT Records, Box 5/ F4.

16 Minutes by Brewer on his meeting with Mackay, November 30, 1968. UNB Archives, AUNBT Records, Box 4/ F15.

17 Minutes of the AUNBT Executive Meeting, December 4, 1968. UNB Archives, AUNBT Records, Box 4/ F15.

18 Brewer to Oliver, December 5, 1968. UNB Archives, AUNBT Records, Box 7/ F1; Hatheway to Brewer, December 16, 1968. UNB Archives, AUNBT Records, Box 7/ F1.

19 "Spades Down" had been selected in 1968 as a preferred title for Tom's column, since it demonstrated more *gravitas* than "Jelly Beans."

20 Interview with Tom Murphy, August 26, 2000.

21 "Spades Down" by Tom Murphy. *Brunswickan*, December 3, 1968, p. 9.

22 Blue to Robertson, November 27, 1968. UNB Archives, Department of Information/Strax Case.

23 Editorial in the *King's County Record*, November 28, 1968.

24 SRC Minutes, December 1, 1968. UNB Archives.

25 Martin journal, November 25–27, 1968.

26 Sharp to Smith, December 11, 1968; Smith to Brewer, December 17, 1968. UNB Archives, AUNBT Records, Box 7/ F1.

27 Interview with R.G.L. Fairweather, August 15, 2002.

28 Robichaud to Mackay, January 3, 1969. UNB Archives, Presidential Papers, S 10, SS 1, 78, F59.

29 Minutes of the Board of Governors, January 16, 1969.

30 Mackay to Robichaud, March 12, 1969. UNB Archives, Presidential Papers, S10, SS1, 78, F59.

31 Martin journal, January 5, 1969.

CHAPTER 7

1 Interview with Ann Cameron, May 2, 2001.

2 Interview with Tom Murphy, August 26, 2000.

3 Interview with John Oliver, August 2, 2002.

4 Memorandum: "Background to the Oliver/Murphy contempt hearings," January 22 to 29, 1969. UNB Archives, H.A. Sharp papers, Series 3, Box 5, F6.

5 Judgment of Justice J. Paul Barry in the case of The University of New Brunswick vs. Norman Strax, December 27, 1968. UNB Archives, President's Papers, S10, SS1, 80, F147.

6 Minutes of the Board of Governors, December 19, 1968. UNB Archives, Bailey Papers/S12, 60, F7.

7 Minutes of the Board of Governors, January 16, 1969.

8 Interview with Alwyn Berland, August 26, 2000.

9 Macpherson to Mackay, January 17, 1969. UNB Archives, AUNBT Records, Box 5, F4.

10 *Rule Nisi* of the Supreme Court of New Brunswick, Appeal Division, December 27, 1968. Archives of the author.

11 Interview with Ann Cameron, May 2, 2001.

12 Interview with Tom Murphy, August 26, 2002.

13 Interview with Alan Borovoy, August 24, 2000.

14 McDonald published the results of her survey and of her experience in Lynn McDonald, "Contempt of Court: An Unsuccessful Attempt to use Sociological Evidence." *Osgoode Hall Law Journal*, Vol. 8, no. 3, 1970. pp. 573–97.

15 Interview with Lynn McDonald, Fredericton, January 30, 2001.

16 Interview with Alan Borovoy, August 24, 2000.

17 SRC Minutes, February 16, 1969.

18 Statement of Resignation by the acting president, February 18, 1969. UNB Archives, Presidential Papers, S10, SS1, 84, F272.

CHAPTER 8

1 Telegram from Macpherson to Mackay, February 10, 1969. UNB Archives, Bailey Papers, S12, 59, F11.

2 Hugo Johnston, *Radical Campus.*

3 Interview with Alwyn Berland, August 26, 2000.

4 Minutes of the Board of Governors, February 20, 1969.

5 Minutes of the Academic Freedom and Tenure meeting, January 11–12, 1969. National Archives, MG 28/Series I 208/Vol. 125, Strax, Norman – UNB – Correspondence – 1969/ Q4-26202.

6 Mackay to Macpherson, February 25, 1969. UNB Archives, Presidential Papers, S9, SS2, 69, F103.

7 Macpherson to Mackay, March 5. 1969, UNB Archives, President's Papers, S10, SS1, 80, F147.

8 Mackay to Macpherson, March 10, 1969. UNB Archives, Presidential Papers, S10, SS1, 80, F147.

9 Sears to Argue, February 24, 1969. UNB Archives, President 59, SS2, 69, F100.

10 Argue to Mackay, March 3, 1969 UNB Archives, President 59, SS2, 69, F100; Mackay to Argue, March 10, 1969. UNB Archives, Argue Papers, Series 1, SS2, Box 4 F66.

11 Minutes of the AUNBT General Meeting, February 7, 1969.

12 Brewer to Smith, February 12, 1969. UNB Archives, AUNBT Papers, Box 7, F1.

13 Minutes of the AUNBT Executive Meeting, February 28, 1969.

14 Brewer to Mackay and Macpherson, March 4, 1969. UNB Archives, AUNBT Papers, Box 7, F1.

15 Telegram from Smith to Brewer, March 3, 1969. UNB Archives, AUNBT Papers, Box 7, F1.

16 Brewer to the AUNBT membership, March 6, 1969. UNB Archives, AUNBT Papers, Box 7, F1.

17 Minutes of the Special Meeting of the AUNBT, March 8, 1969. UNB Archives, AUNBT Papers, Box 5, F4.

18 AUNBT Executive to Mackay, March 9, 1969. UNB Archives, Presidential Papers, S10, SS1, 80, F145.

19 Judgment in the case of the Queen and Thomas Raymond Murphy, March 12, 1969. Papers in the author's possession.

20 Interview with Tom Murphy, August 26, 2000.

21 SRC Minutes, January 26, 1969.

22 SRC Minutes, February 16, 1969.

23 SRC Minutes, February 23, 1969.

24 Harper to Sharp, January 17, 1969. UNB Archives, H.A. Sharp papers, Series 3, Box 5, F6. The total bill came to $1,004.75, but deducting $300 already paid, the balance owing was $704.75. The invoice was made jointly to the Academic Freedom Fund, c/o Harold Sharp, and to John Oliver, with Harper indicating that he would not expect Oliver to pay "more than $100.00 to $150.00."

25 Harper to Macpherson, March 3, 1969. UNB Archives, H.A. Sharp papers, Series 3, Box 5, F6.

26 Minutes of the AUNBT Executive Meeting, March 12, 1969, UNB Archives, AUNBT Papers, Box 4, F15.

27 AUNBT Executive to Robinson, March 12, 1969. UNB Archives, AUNBT Papers, Box 7, F1.

28 Chapman to Robinson, March 14, 1969. UNB Archives, AUNBT Papers, Box 7, F1.

29 Dick Wilbur, "Shop Talk," March 14, 1969. UNB Archives, Department of Information, Strax Case 1969.

30 Minutes of the Meeting of the CAUT Council, March 15, 1969. UNB Archives, Harold Sharp Papers, series 3, box 5, F6; speech by W.C. Desmond Pacey at the CAUT Council, March 15, 1969. National Archives of Canada, MG28/ Series I 208/ Volume 125.

CHAPTER 9

1 Hatheway to Alan Pacey, March 19, 1969. UNB Archives, Department of Information/Strax Case.

2 Interview with Michael Start, December 27, 2000.

3 Interview with Lawson Hunter, August 7, 2000; interview with David Jonah, August 15, 2000.

4 Report by Special SRC Committee on Effects of Possible CAUT Censure on UNB, March 9, 1969. UNB Archives, SRC Minutes, 1969 January–March; SRC Minutes, March 9, 1969.

5 *Brunswickan*, February 7, 1969.

6 Martin journal, January 27–February 17, 1969.

7 Minutes of the AUNBT Meeting, March 18, 1969; AUNBT Resolution, March 18, 1969. UNB Archives, Bailey Papers, 80, F22.

8 Turner to Mackay, March 17, 1969. UNB Archives, Presidential Papers, S10, SS1, 78, F61.

9 Sergeant to Mackay, March 20, 1969. UNB Archives, Presidential Papers, S9, SS2, 69, F101

10 Pinet to Robichaud, March 17, 1969. UNB Archives, Presidential Papers, S10, SS1, 78, F59.

11 Harrison Trimble High School teachers to Mackay, April 1, 1969. UNB Archives, Presidential Papers, S9, SS2, 69, F101.

12 Macpherson to Mackay, March 17, 1969. UNB Archives, Bailey Papers, 80, F22.

13 Robichaud to Mackay, March 19, 1969. UNB Archives, Presidential Papers, S10, SS1, 80, F147.

14 Macpherson to Robinson, March 20, 1969. UNB Archives, AUNBT Papers, Box 7, F1.

15 SRC Minutes, March 16, 1969.

16 Start to Mackay, March 18, 1969. UNB Archives, Presidential Papers, S10, SS1, 84, F272.

17 Martin journal, March 9–20, 1969.

18 Minutes of the SRC Administrative Board, March 8, 1969.

19 Interview with Les Shemilt, August 26, 2000.

20 Minutes of the Board of Governors, March 20, 1969. UNB Archives, Bailey Papers, S12, 59, F11.

21 *Telegraph-Journal*, March 20, 1969.

22 Interview with Dan Weston, August 23, 2002.

23 *Telegraph-Journal*, March 21, 1969.

24 Interview with Dan Weston, August 23, 2002.

25 *Telegraph-Journal*, March 21, 1969.

26 Black to Mackay, March 21, 1969. UNB Archives, Presidential Papers, S9, SS2, 69, F101.

27 Cox to the Chairman of the Board of Governors, March 21, 1969. UNB Archives, Presidential Papers, S9, SS2, 69, F101.

28 Ganong to the Chairman of the Board of Governors, March 24, 1969. UNB Archives, Presidential Papers, S9, SS2, 69, F101.

29 Mackay to Robichaud, March 21, 1969. UNB Archives, Presidential Papers, S10, SS1, 78, F59.

30 The CAUT censure of the President and Board of Governors of Simon Fraser University in May 1968, which resulted in the firing of President McTaggart-Cowan. This was the first time that CAUT had applied censure to any university.

31 Mackay to Turner, March 21, 1969. UNB Archives, Presidential Papers, S10, SS1, 78, F61.

32 Mackay to Sargeant, March 24, 1969. UNB Archives, Presidential Papers, S9, SS2, 69, F101.

CHAPTER 10

1 Notes by Robinson, March 27, 1969, UNB Archives, AUNBT Papers, Box 7, F2.

2 Interview with Alwyn Berland, August 26, 2000.

3 Boone to Strax, March 29, 1969. UNB Archives, Presidential Papers S9, SS2, 69, F100.

4 Questions raised by Strax and Memorandum by Robinson, April 1969. UNB Archives, AUNBT Papers, Box 7, F2.

5 Notes by Robinson, April 5, 1969. UNB Archives, AUNBT Papers, Box 7, F2.

6 Transcript of tape by Mackay, April 11, 1969. UNB Archives, Presidential Papers, S9, SS2, 69, F100.

7 Macpherson to Mackay, April 12, 1969. UNB Archives, Presidential Papers, S9, SS2, 69, F103.

8 Minutes of the Board of Governors, April 22, 1969.

9 Agreement between the CAUT and UNB, May 1, 1969. UNB Archives, Presidential Papers, S10, SS1, 80, F147.

10 Minutes of the Board of Governors, May 14, 1969.

11 Transcript of UNB v. Norman Strax before J. Paul Barry, May 16, 1969. UNB Archives, Bailey Papers, S12, 59, F11.

12 Nicholson to Berland, May 20, 1969. UNB Archives, Harold Sharp Papers, Series 3, Box 5, F6.

13 Macpherson to Mackay, May 21, 1969, UNB Archives, Presidential Papers, S9, SS2, 69, F103.

14 Mackay to Smith, May 22, 1969. UNB Archives. Presidential Papers, S9, SS2, 69, F103.

15 CAUT Press Release, May 23, 1969. UNB Archives, Presidential Papers, S9, SS2, 69, F103.

16 Notes by Unger, after May 20, 1969. UNB Archives, AUNBT Papers, Box 7, F1.

17 Macpherson to Mackay, May 27, 1969. UNB Archives, Bailey Papers, 80, F22.

18 Allen to Mackay, June 2, 1969. UNB Archives, Bailey Papers, 80, F22.

19 Mackay to Hoyt, June 6, 1969. UNB Archives, Presidential Papers, S10, SS1, 80, F147.

20 Minutes of the Board of Governors, June 20, 1969.

21 Mackay to Macpherson, June 21, 1969; Macpherson to Mackay, June 25, 1969; Mackay to Macpherson, June 30, 1969. UNB Archives, Presidential Papers, S10, SS1, 80, F147.

22 Dineen to Berland July 18, 1969. UNB Archives, Presidential Papers, S10, SS1, 80, F147.

23 Berland to Dineen, July 18, 1969. UNB Archives, Presidential Papers, S10, SS1, 80, F147.

24 McAllister to Palmer, May 1, 1969. UNB Archives, Presidential Papers, S10, SS1, 80, F147.

25 Mackay to Meagher, May 9, 1969. UNB Archives, Presidential Papers, S10, SS1, 80, F147

26 Palmer to Pacholke, July 3, 1969. UNB Archives, Presidential Papers, S10, SS1, 80, F147.

27 Pacholke to Palmer, July 31, 1969. UNB Archives, Presidential Papers, S10, SS1, 80, F147.

28 Strax to Dineen, August 1, 1969. UNB Archives, Presidential Papers, S10, SS1, 80, F147.

29 Palmer to Berland, August 20, 1969. UNB Archives, Bailey Papers, 80, F22. Much of the description of the arbitration process is drawn from Palmer's letter.

30 McAllister to Strax, August 21, 1969. UNB Archives, Bailey Papers, 80, F22.

31 Dineen to Strax, August 26, 1969. UNB Archives, Presidential Papers, S10, SS1, 80, F147.

32 Memo by Dineen, August 27, 1969. UNB Archives, Presidential Papers, S10, SS1, 80, F147.

33 Berland to Dineen, September 2, 1969. UNB Archives, Presidential Papers, S10, SS1, 80, F147.

34 Mahan to Berland, September 10, 1969. UNB Archives, Papers of the Comptroller, Box 24, F3; Monahan to Mahan, October 1, 1969. UNB Archives, Papers of the Comptroller, Box 24, F3.

35 Mackay to Palmer, September 4, 1969. UNB Archives, Presidential Papers, S10, SS1, 80, F147.

CHAPTER 11

1 AUCC Press Release, April 18, 1969. UNB Archives, Department of Information, Strax Case 1969.

2 Atkinson to Mackay, June 2, 1969. UNB Archives, Presidential Papers, S9, SS2, 69, F100.

3 Saunderson to Allen, June 9, 1969. UNB Archives, Bailey Papers, 80, F22.

4 Mackay to Bailey, June 24, 1969. UNB Archives, Presidential Papers, S10, SS1, 85, F322.

5 Minutes of the Board of Deans, September 3, 1969. UNB Archives, Bailey Papers, S12, 60, F6.

6 Interview with Lawson Hunter, August 7, 2000; Interview with Gordon Fairweather, August 15, 2002.

Lawson Hunter later became Assistant Deputy Minister at Industry Canada and was responsible for the drafting of the federal *Competition Act* before moving on to become a partner in the law firm Stikeman Elliott, and subsequently executive vice-president and chief corporate officer of Bell Canada and BCE Inc. In 2011, Hunter was awarded an honorary degree by the University of New Brunswick.

7 Patterson to Mackay, March 25, 1969; Minutes of the SCM Advisory Board, June 24, 1969; Patterson to Wilson, March 23, 1970, Patterson Papers.

8 SCM Press Release, June 1, 1970, Patterson Papers; Interview with Tom Murphy, August 26, 2000; see also Gidney, "Poisoning the Student Mind?" pp. 147–63; Robin Boyd, *The Witness of the Student Christian Movement: Church Ahead of the Church*. London: SPCK, 2007.

9 Tom Murphy subsequently became a professor at the University of Western Ontario.

10 Glenda Turner, *James Owen Dineen: Profile of an Engineering Educator*. APENB and UNB, 2000, p. 76.

11 Minutes of the Board of Deans, September 3, 1969. UNB Archives, Bailey Papers, S12, 60, F6.

12 *University Gazette*, Vol. 1, no. 1, September 17, 1969.

13 Correspondence with Thomas J. Condon, Dean of Arts in the 1970s, February 20, 2011.

14 "University Security Organization — Policy," October 6, 1969. UNB Archives, Minutes of the SRC, 1969 September–December.

15 Minutes of the University Committee, November 26, 1969. UNB Archives, Bailey Papers, Case 82, F2.

16 Interview with Stephen Patterson, August 17, 2000.

17 Turner, *James Owen Dineen*, p. 77.

18 Interview with Les Shemilt, August 26, 2000.

19 James Downey was president of UNB from 1980 to 1990 and president of the University of Waterloo from 1993 to 1999.

20 Interview with Alwyn Berland, August 26, 2000.

21 Minutes of the AUNBT AGM, April 22, 1969. UNB Archives, AUNBT Papers, Box 5, F4.

22 Minutes of a Special AUNBT Executive meeting, June 2, 1969. UNB Archives, AUNBT Papers, Box 4, F15; Minutes of the AUNBT Special Information Meeting, July 2, 1969. UNB Archives, AUNBT Papers, Box 5, F4.

23 Professional faculty members to Unger, December 4, 1969. UNB Archives, AUNBT Papers, Box 4, F15.

24 In 1969–70, Business Administration was a department in the Faculty of Arts.

25 Minutes of the AUNBT Executive Committee meetings on December 15 and December 18, 1969. UNB Archives, AUNBT Papers, Box 4, F15.

26 During Jim Downey's decade as UNB president from 1980 to 1990, he deliberately refused to consider implementing any kind of strategic planning exercise.

27 Correspondence with Thomas J. Condon, February 20, 2011.

28 "Historical Notes on AUNBT." http://aunbt.caut.ca/history.html

29 Peter McGahan, *The "Quiet Campus": A History of the University of New Brunswick in Saint John, 1959–1969*. Saint John: New Ireland Press, 1998.

30 Detached from the university, Strax sought out other examples of institutional injustice. On July 20, 1969, according to a broadsheet handed out by one of his followers, "Willard Parsons — a 55 year-old coal miner, with only one arm and a serious lung disease was arrested and beaten by a policeman for 'intoxication.'" Strax had been taking pictures of the policeman while he was making the arrest, and now, the broadsheet went on:

...the Crown Prosecutor is demanding that Strax be convicted and jailed for up to two years as punishment for taking these pictures. (The Prosecutor claims that taking photographs is 'obstructing a police officer.') The court has refused to allow Strax to be defended by the lawyer of his choice (Mr. Clayton Ruby, of Toronto). Thus Strax has had to defend himself, without a lawyer.

People were invited to come to the trial on Tuesday, October 14.

If the Prosecutor succeeds in this frame-up trial it will establish a very dangerous precedent. — You will never again be able to take a photograph of a policeman unless he first gives you his permission. Defend your right to criticize the police when they are in the wrong. (Handout sheet, "Come to the Trial," October 14, 1969, UNB Archives, Presidential Papers, S10, SS1, 80, F145).

Strax, apparently, was convicted of harassment and of obstructing the work of the police and proceedings were initiated for his deportation from Canada but these were overturned on appeal. (Berland to McDiarmid, June 2, 1970, National Archives/ MG28/ Series I 208/ Vol. 98 "Strax Professor — correspondence 1967–70" QU-25605).

31 Interview with Dan Weston, August 23, 2002.

Within the Fredericton community, Strax was seen as a sinister figure around whose name legends were woven, and his appearance on a downtown street was an occasion of note to those who saw him. In 1969 Strax and a number of his followers took up the issue of the "people's park." 1968 and 1969 were the years of the arrival of "hippie culture" in Fredericton, with many young people hitch-hiking their way across the country and finding places to sleep rough when they landed in towns and cities along the way. To control these groups of young people, the Fredericton City Council established a curfew, which led to the police throwing young people off the riverside green when they were there after hours. In response, Dan Weston and others decided to "liberate" Officer's Square on Queen Street by occupying it as a "people's park." Once about fifteen young people had gathered with a guitar, they found they attracted a large and hostile crowd who began throwing smoke bombs and lighted paper bags. When some of the young people's hair was catching fire, they decided to leave and formed a "flying wedge" to push through the crowd to run back to one of the co-op residences. That ended the "people's park" demonstration.

BIBLIOGRAPHY

PRIMARY SOURCES
National Archives of Canada
Papers of the Canadian Association of University Teachers (CAUT)

Archives of the University of New Brunswick
Presidential Papers
Minutes of the Board of Governors
Report of the Commission on the Future of the University, January 1, 1967
Minutes of the Student's Representative Council
Calendars, 1953–1969
Papers of the Office of the Comptroller
Papers of the University Librarian
Papers of the Department of Information
Records of the Association of University of New Brunswick Teachers (AUNBT)
C.W. Argue Papers
Alfred G. Bailey Papers
Harold A. Sharp Papers
Barry Toole Papers
Miscellaneous papers relating to the Strax Affair

Private Collections
Peter C. Kent Papers
Tom Murphy Papers
Stephen Patterson Papers

Interviews
Alwyn Berland, Hamilton, ON, August 26, 2000
Alan Borovoy, Toronto, ON, August 24, 2000
Ann Cameron, Fredericton, May 2, 2001
David Cox (with Diana Cox), Toronto, ON, August 24, 2000
Kenneth V. Cox, by telephone, August 12, 2000
John Earl, Fredericton, June 20, 2002
R.G.L. Fairweather, Kingston Peninsula, NB, August 15, 2002
Gertrude Gunn, Fredericton, June 17, 2002

Lawson Hunter, Fredericton, August 7, 2000
David Jonah, Moncton, August 15, 2000
Lynn McDonald, Fredericton, January 20, 2001
Tom Murphy, London, ON, August 26, 2000
John Oliver, Toronto, ON, August 2, 2002
Stephen Patterson, Fredericton, August 17, 2000
Marion Rogers, Rothesay, November 20, 1993
Harold Sharp, Fredericton, August 14, 2000
Leslie Shemilt, Hamilton, ON, August 26, 2000
Michael Start, Fredericton, December 27, 2000
Dan Weston, Fredericton, August 23, 2002
D.M. Young, Fredericton, June 7, 2002

Memoirs and Journals
Martin, Franz. Unpublished journal for 1968–69.
Murray, Thomas A. "Some Remembrances and Thoughts on My Participation in the Strax Affair, Fredericton, New Brunswick, 1968." Unpublished manuscript.
Savoie, Donald J. *I'm from Bouctouche, Me: Roots Matter*, Montreal and Kingston: McGill-Queen's University Press, 2009.
Tweedie, R.A. *On With The Dance: A New Brunswick Memoir 1935–1960*, Saint John: New Ireland Press, 1986.

SECONDARY SOURCES
Anderson, Terry H. *The Movement and the Sixties: Protest in America from Greensboro to Wounded Knee.* New York: Oxford University Press, 1995.
Axelrod, Paul. *Scholars and Dollars: Politics, Economics and Universities of Ontario, 1945–1980.* Toronto: University of Toronto Press, 1982.
———. *Values in Conflict: The University, the Marketplace, and the Trials of Liberal Education.* Montreal & Kingston: McGill-Queen's University Press, 2002.
Axelrod, Paul, and John Reid (eds.). *Youth, University and Canadian Society: Essays in the Social History of Higher Education.* Montreal & Kingston: McGill-Queen's University Press, 1989.
Barber, David. *A Hard Rain Fell: SDS and Why it Failed.* Jackson: University Press of Mississippi, 2008.
Berton, Pierre. *1967: The Last Good Year.* Toronto: Doubleday Canada Ltd., 1997.
Boyd, Robin. *The Witness of the Student Christian Movement: Church ahead of the Church.* London: SPCK, 2007.
Braddock, John. "Strife on Campus," *The Atlantic Advocate*, May 1969, pp. 18–25.
Burner, David. *Making Peace with the 60s.* Princeton: Princeton University Press, 1996.
Cameron, David M. *More Than an Academic Question: Universities, Government, and Public Policy in Canada.* Halifax: Institute for Research on Public Policy, 1991.
C.A.U.T. Bulletin.

Charters, David. "Propaganda and the Strax Crisis." Unpublished manuscript, 1978.

Cormier, Michel. *Louis J. Robichaud: A Not So Quiet Revolution*. Translated by Jonathan Kaplansky. Moncton: Faye Editions, 2004.

Couturier, Jacques Paul. *Construire un savoir: l'enseignement supérieur au Madawaska, 1946–1974*. Moncton: Les Editions d'Acadie, 1999.

Eber, Dorothy. *The Computer Centre Party: Canada Meets Black Power*. Montreal: Tundra Books, 1969.

Farquharson, Duart. "Confrontation on the Campus." Collected articles for the Southam Press, January 1969.

Forbes, E.R. and D.A. Muise. *The Atlantic Provinces in Confederation*. Toronto: University of Toronto Press, and Fredericton: Acadiensis Press, 1993.

Gidney, Catherine. "Poisoning the Student Mind?: The Student Christian Movement at the University of Toronto, 1920–1965." *Journal of the Canadian Historical Association*, 1997, New Series, Vol. 8, pp. 147–63.

———. "The Canadian Association of University Teachers and the Rise of Faculty Power, 1951–70." Unpublished manuscript.

———. "War and the Concept of Generation: The International Teach-Ins at the University of Toronto, 1965–1968." Unpublished manuscript.

Horn, Michiel. *Academic Freedom in Canada: A History*. Toronto: University of Toronto Press, 1999.

Interesting Times: A Newsletter from AUNBT, Fall 2008.

Johnston, Hugo. *Radical Campus: Making Simon Fraser University*. Vancouver: Douglas and McIntyre, 2005.

Kent, Peter C. "Conflicting Conceptions of Rights in UNB's Strax Affair, 1968–69," *University of New Brunswick Law Journal*, Vol. 44, 1995, pp. 87–91.

———. "The Contextual Significance of UNB's Strax Affair." Paper presented to the Atlantic Canada Studies Conference XIII, Mount St. Vincent University, May 5, 2000.

———. "The Unrealized Potential of Canada's Universities." *Acadiensis*, Vol. 31, no. 2 (Spring 2002).

Kostash, Myrna. *Long Way from Home: The Story of the Sixties Generation in Canada*. Toronto: James Lorimer and Company, 1980.

Kurlansky, Mark. *1968: The Year that Rocked the World*. New York: Random House, 2004.

Levi, Charles Morden. *Comings and Goings: University Students in Canadian Society, 1854–1973*. Montreal and Kingston: McGill-Queen's University Press, 2003.

Levitt, Cyril. *Children of Privilege: Student Revolt in the Sixties, A Study of Student Movements in Canada, the United States and West Germany*. Toronto: University of Toronto Press, 1984.

Lexier, Roberta. "The Community of Scholars: The English-Canadian Student Movement and University Governance." In Marie Hammond-Callaghan and Matthew Hayday (eds.). *Mobilizations, Protests and Engagements: Canadian Perspectives on Social Movements*. Halifax and Winnipeg: Fernwood Publishing, 2008, pp. 125–44.

Makin, Kirk. "Farewell to Canada's top freedom fighter." *The Globe and Mail*, April 25, 2009.

McDonald, Lynn. "Contempt of Court: An Unsuccessful Attempt to use Sociological Evidence." *Osgoode Hall Law Journal*, Vol. 8, no. 3, 1970, pp. 573–97.

McGahan, Peter. *The 'Quiet Campus': A History of the University of New Brunswick in Saint John, 1959–1969*. Fredericton: New Ireland Press, 1998.

McNaught, Kenneth. *Conscience and History: A Memoir*. Toronto: University of Toronto Press, 1999.

Mendell, David. *Obama: From Promise to Power*. New York: Amistad, 2007

Montague, Susan. *A Pictorial History of the University of New Brunswick*. Fredericton: University of New Brunswick, 1992.

Murphy, Tom. "Spades Down." *Brunswickan*, December 3, 1968.

Owram, Doug. *Born at the Right Time: A History of the Baby-Boom Generation*. Toronto: University of Toronto Press, 1996.

Palmer, Bryan D. *Canada's 1960s: The Ironies of Identity in a Rebellious Era*. Toronto: University of Toronto Press, 2009.

Pasolli, Lisa. "Bureaucratizing the Atlantic Revolution: The 'Saskatchewan Mafia' in the New Brunswick Civil Service, 1960–1970." *Acadiensis* Vol. 38, no. 1 (Winter/Spring 2009), pp. 126–50.

Reid, John G. *Mount Allison University: A History, to 1963, Volume II: 1914–1963*. Toronto: University of Toronto Press, 1984.

———. "Some Historical Reflections on the Report of the Royal Commission on Higher Education in New Brunswick, 1962." Unpublished manuscript, 1989.

Reid, Tim and Julyan (eds.). *Student Power and the Canadian Campus*. Toronto: Peter Martin Associates, Ltd., 1969.

Shook, Laurence K. *Catholic post-secondary education in English-speaking Canada: A History*. Toronto: University of Toronto Press, 1971.

Stanley, Della M.M. *Louis Robichaud: A Decade of Power*. Halifax: Nimbus Publishing Limited, 1984.

Stewart, LaVerne. "Selfless Dedication." *The Daily Gleaner*, July 26, 2008, pp. E1–E2.

Tudiver, Neil. *Universities for Sale: Resisting Corporate Control over Canadian Higher Education*. Toronto: James Lorimer and Company, 1999.

Turk, James (ed.). *The Corporate Campus: Commercialization and the Dangers to Canada's Colleges and Universities*. Toronto: James Lorimer and Company Ltd., 2000.

Turner, Glenda. *James Owen Dineen: Profile of an Engineering Educator*. Fredericton: Association of Professional Engineers and Geoscientists of New Brunswick and the Faculty of Engineering of the University of New Brunswick, 2000.

Veniot, André. "The pinstriped revolutionary: Ed Byrne and the inside story of Equal Opportunity." *The New Brunswick Reader Magazine*, October 23, 1999, pp. 16–19.

Waite, P.B. *The Lives of Dalhousie University, Volume Two, 1925–1980*, "The Old College Transformed." Montreal and Kingston: McGill-Queen's University Press, 1998.

Winter, Hal. "The strange case of doctor Norman Strax or how 'protesting' was started at old UNB." *The Gazette*, Montreal, November 9, 1968.

The Press and Other Media
The Atlantic Advocate, Fredericton, NB
The *Brunswickan*, UNB
The Daily Gleaner, Fredericton, NB
The Gazette, Montreal, QC
The Globe and Mail
King's County Record, Sussex, NB
The Mysterious East
New York Times
Princeton Alumni Web Page
Telegraph-Journal, Saint John, NB
University Gazette, UNB

IMAGE CREDITS

INDEX